CLOSER

THAN YOU

THINK

SIX FUNDAMENTAL QUESTIONS TO IGNITE YOUR
PERSONAL EVOLUTION

MIKE MERRIAM

Print ISBN: 978-0-9979692-1-4

Digital ISBN: Book: 978-0-9979692-0-7

Interior Design by Christina Culbertson, 3CsBooks.com

DEDICATION

This book is dedicated my wife and best friend, Melissa Merriam. You've remained by my side through the good times and the tough times, and have always believed in me. You've helped me remain rooted and avoid the hazards of my big dreams, while quietly co-piloting my trajectory to the person who can now realize those dreams. I suspect that I would be a shadow of myself without you. I love you and believe in you. My most earnest hope is that I will have the ability to add just a fraction of the value to your life that you have added to mine.

A SPECIAL INVITATION

You are cordially invited to join our growing private tribe of Radical Visioneers, thought-leaders, and like-minded personal evolutionaries, all dedicated to massively transformative futures.

Just go to https://www.facebook.com/groups/personalevolutiontribe/ and request to join.

This book is evergreen, meaning it lives electronically online. Because of this, it can be updated at any time. I'm hoping we can work together to update it in the future.

I'm inviting you to join me in answering the following questions:

1. What would it look like if this book became *the book* to achieve a radically transformative future filled with unlimited happiness and fulfillment?

2. How could we add to, subtract from, and/or adapt this book so that it becomes the *ultimate guide* and *go-to resource?*

I'm inviting you to join me in answering these questions and making this a reality. I'm looking forward to seeing you in the *Personal Evolution Tribe.* I'm committed to collaborating in an effort to build great ideas, work to improve lives, and change the world together.

I have a vision to change the world one Personal Evolution at a time. Will you join me?

CONTENTS

INTRODUCTION: A Special Invitation i

Why I Wrote This Book and What I Hope it Accomplishes v

Adaptation Sparks Evolution xi

The Six Fundamental Questions xiii

The Art and Science of Personal Evolution xxi

Background Part 1: My Call to Action 1

Background Part 2: The Personal Evolution Revolution 9

Evolutionary Truths: Foundational Principals 17

CHAPTER 1: 19
Now is the Time to Leave the Unhappy,
Unfulfilled, & Disengaged Majority Behind

CHAPTER 2: 25
Greatness Demands Positivity

CHAPTER 3: 34
Fundamental Question #1—What Are
My Core Values (And Why)?

CHAPTER 4: 41
How Language and Emotions Create Reality

CHAPTER 5: 47
Fundamental Question #2—What Are
My Unique Strengths?

CHAPTER 6: 52

Choose Your Reactions—The Synapses
That Fire Together Wire Together

CHAPTER 7: 60

From Unfulfilled to Unlimited: Eliminate Fear and
Curate Abundance Through Courage and Curiosity

CHAPTER 8: 69

Fundamental Question #3—What Are My
Priorities and Motivations?

CHAPTER 9: 74

Fundamental Question #4—What Might a
Radical Vision of a Truly Fulfilling Life Look Like?

CHAPTER 10: 80

Fundamental Question #5—Why Would
My Radical Vision Look Like That?

CHAPTER 11: 84

Fundamental Question #6—How Might
I go About Designing My Radical, Fulfilling Life?

CHAPTER 12: 93

Maintaining the Change—The AVID Practice

Wrap up and Next Steps 101

The Radical Vision 30-Day Challenge 104

Contact Me if I Can Add Value 108

Bonus Materials—Goal Setting Framework 110

Acknowledgments 118

WHY I WROTE THIS BOOK & WHAT I HOPE IT ACCOMPLISHES

One of the most popular and regrettably true quotes of all time is by Henry David Thoreau, who said, "The mass of men lead lives of quiet desperation and go to the grave with the song still in them." What he meant is, the vast majority of people are unhappy, unfulfilled, and disengaged. This sad fact is evidenced by numerous studies and polls, conducted by top universities, Gallop, and Deloitte, that confirm this to be true. If this represents you, don't fret, because I believe something entirely different. I believe that you are just a couple of learned skills, a couple of big realizations, and a couple of key connections away from revolutionizing your life. That's why I wrote this book.

I believe that regardless of where you are today, you are much closer than you think to revolutionizing your life. You may sense that you are indeed close, perhaps you just need a refresher. Or maybe you feel light-years away and entirely lost. I can assure you that's not the case. You just haven't asked the right questions and learned to answer them properly. By the end of this book and the corresponding online course, The Personal Evolution Plan, you will have mapped your Positive Core, designed a Radical Vision for the future, and will have all of the tools and knowledge necessary to manifest that vision into reality.

Wherever you are on the pathway of life, this book is your guide to a radically transformative future, should you choose it.

I encourage you to treat the reading of this book as a "choose your own adventure" roadmap for your life. Please understand right now before we get started, that you can go anywhere that's possible for you to go. You can be anyone that it's possible for you to be. I use the word "possible" because obviously there are some places we cannot go, and some things we cannot be by our very nature and the nature of life. However, it doesn't matter what baggage you have, who you're responsible for, or what you've done in the past. You can still evolve. When was the last time you reminded yourself of this fact? It's important to accept this as the truth, because it is. Your rearview mirror is your enemy, not your guiding light. Don't look back. Your north star is within you and will be unlocked, if you commit to participating fully in this book and with the Personal Evolution Plan.

I challenge you to put your limiting beliefs (a.k.a. your fears and excuses) aside for the remainder of these pages. Just as an exercise in what you're capable of, do yourself the great favor of reading this book with an open mind and a can-do attitude. No, a *will-do* attitude! If you do this, I promise your life will never be the same.

The Navy Seals use something they call the 40 percent rule. When they feel they have reached their limit and can't take any more of the grueling demands placed upon them, they are reminded that in fact they are only at 40 percent of their real potential and have 60 percent more to give if they dig deep. This is how the Seals accomplish what seem like superhuman feats. Find your inner seal and refuse to fail.

You've probably been asked the following question before: "If money were no object, what would you do with your life?"

Maybe you answered that you'd travel the world, start a charity, write a book, or start a business. Perhaps something else? I've studied thousands of answers to this question, and people overwhelmingly respond within one of two categories. That is, they would either start a business or do something to help people and animals.

These anecdotes show that what most people want more than anything in life is to have the luxury of experiencing firsthand what I call the elevating human needs of *growth* and *contribution*. They are elevating needs because, when satisfied, they lead us to evolve. They lead us to true happiness and fulfillment, and what I believe is the meaning of life. We'll talk more about this and other basic needs in Chapter 2. For now, just understand that these two elevating human needs, *growth* and *contribution*, are what we all desire and would focus on if our other needs could be suitably met.

I wrote this book to show you how to do this right now and teach you to love the life you are living while you build the life of your dreams. I want you to leave your life as a member of the unhappy, unfulfilled, and disengaged majority behind, and design your own Personal Evolution!

A NOTE TO YOU, THE READER

As I write this note to you, it's been nearly one year since I began this book. So much has happened over the past year that's led me to a place of joy and fulfillment, but there's so much more personal work to be done. I want to share what I've learned with you before you get into the heart of this book. I'm writing this note exactly one week before publication. As soon as I get to the bottom of the page, I'll be hitting the send button and off the manuscript will go for formatting and publishing.

Throughout this work, you'll hear me talk about developing a mindset of abundance, eliminating negativity and turning limits into empowerments. You'll hear me discuss how fear is our greatest enemy and how we should all use fear as an indication of what we *should* do. How we should run towards fear and face it head on.

I want to point out that I understand this is easier said than done. In fact, right now in my life, I'm struggling every day to practice what I preach. Let me explain.

Throughout this book, you'll hear me talk a lot about creating a *Radical Vision* and following that vision by allowing the best of you, your positive core, to lead your actions. To allow the emerging future guide you today.

My radical vision for the future is writing this book, and building a coaching and consulting business where I can help people and organizations map their positive cores, design radical, transformative visions, and be integral to the evolution of society. Out of necessity, as I have a family, a home, and bills to pay, I've had to keep this as my *side hustle.* My passion project made possible by my regular, full-time job in the mortgage banking industry.

Three weeks ago I lost that job.

I'm telling you this because nothing has tested my resolve and my commitment to living in alignment with the messages in this book more than the recent events in my life have. The income that I lost was significant, and it was necessary.

I had a choice to make. I could go out and get another mortgage job, or I could choose to see what had happened as an opportunity to pursue my passions full-time. To quote the old Cortez reference, my boats were burned. I could either rebuild them and retreat, or see this as a point of no return and either conquer or die. I choose to conquer! Yes, this is a little dramatic, but hey, that's how I roll.

For the past three weeks it's been a constant internal struggle, back and forth. Feelings of self-doubt, self-pity, worry, anxiety, and anger have all emerged and subsided. Each time, I've leaned into the approaches, methods, challenges, and ideas that I write about in this book to give me the strength to follow my heart, to conquer my goals. To overcome the negativity.

I'm sharing this with you because when I wrote this book, it was easy for me to say all of the things I said. Life was easy and I didn't have much to worry about. Now however, as I head into the holidays and the new year having to create my own future without a regular pay check, it's not as easy. What it is however, is more important than ever.

You may be experiencing your own hardships and anxiety, or perhaps you're living though one of the easier periods of life at the moment. Wherever you currently find yourself, one thing is certain....You won't remain there for very long. Life changes.

I want to express to you that I understand how difficult it can be to remain positive when you're worried. How tough it can be to lead with the best of yourself when you're stressed. It's incredibly difficult but it's literally the most important thing you can do for yourself and for your future. I challenge you to read the following pages keeping this in mind.

I commit to you that I will always be transparent and authentic in my communications. I hope that in sharing this story you'll see this commitment and hopefully take some inspiration from it. I'd love to connect and share my emerging future story with you, and be a part of yours. Please reach out if I can add value to your life in any way. Most importantly, lean into the content of this book when life is easy and when it's hard. It will always give you exactly what you need. I say this from personal experience. I say this as I'm practicing what I preach.

Gratefully,

Mike Merriam

ADAPTATION SPARKS EVOLUTION

Any evolution requires adaptation. That is to say, to improve core functions. Adaptations in nature are the result of natural selection. When it comes to human emotions and psychology, however, it's not so simple. In order for us to adapt in a way that improves how we function in our lives, we have to choose what we focus on. Once we choose what to focus on, we have to use our focus to change our behavior. Once our behavior changes, our lives begin to evolve.

There are three main components to completing a personal evolution.

First, cause a change in behavior.

Second, sustain that change.

Third, know the end game.

The main reason personal development books and programs don't work for people is because they fail to do two things. First, show people how to build their own foundation for growth, and second, provide a personalized framework to grow within. What I mean by this is that almost all personal development books are written from the author's perspective, and while they contain lessons and shortcuts that can save you time and help you avoid mistakes, they're only providing a Band-Aid approach to change.

Just as you cannot build a house without a foundation and a frame, neither can you build the best version of yourself without taking the time to answer Six Fundamental Questions that become your foundation for growth. In the final chapter you will learn about my daily AVID practice which acts as your framework to grow within. These tools work symbiotically to help create your Personal Evolution.

THE SIX FUNDAMENTAL QUESTIONS

1. What are my core values (and why)?

2. What are my unique strengths?

3. What are my top priorities and motivations?

4. What might a radical vision of a truly fulfilling life look like?

5. Why would my radical vision look like that?

6. How might I go about designing my radical, fulfilling life?

Yes I know this seems extremely simple, but when explored intentionally, with a focus on obtaining a deep contextual understanding, the answers to these questions can be used to revolutionize your life. Remember, it's not having the knowledge of where your destination is that gets you there; it's pounding the pavement to actually arrive.

Once you answer these questions, it's time to take action. Taking measured, intentional, and essential action is what will catalyze you to make a quantum leap from your current life trajectory to a truly transformative future.

Measured, in the sense that you are analyzing your results and outcomes to ensure the right actions are being taken. This involves daily reflection and self-questioning. The goal is always to analyze, adapt, and overcome.

Intentional, meaning your actions are directed to obtain a *specific outcome,* and that you have clarity on what that outcome is. Many of our efforts are wasted because we are not clear on our desired outcomes. This is where it's important to trust your gut. Many of us ignore or underestimate the power of our gut reaction and underlying emotional responses. If it doesn't feel right, then it's probably not something you actually desire.

Essential, in that your actions are not being taken in vain by focusing on the 80 percent of life that is non-essential to driving desired outcomes. But rather your efforts are effecting the 20 percent of life that actually matters. The sooner you learn and practice this, the better life will become.

THE ART AND SCIENCE OF
PERSONAL EVOLUTION

The psychology and methodologies of the life-changing practices you'll learn in this book are based upon, and rooted in, evidence-based principles and techniques derived from cutting-edge neuroscience, positive psychology, neurolinguistic programming, appreciative inquiry, and personal experience. Their purpose is to empower you to remove the limits from your life by changing your story, taking a strengths-based approach to designing your future, discovering your hero within, and interrupting the patterns that keep you from living the life of your dreams.

RADICAL VISIONING

Radical Visioning is nothing more than the intentional design of the future based upon the absolute best of what is and what has been. It flows from the systematic discovery (Six Fundamental Questions) of what drives people when they are at their most capable, effective, clear, and determined. When they are free from limiting forces and compelled by their desire for growth and contribution to persevere.

The phrase Radical Visioning means to fundamentally change the mental image of your future. To see yourself living an abundant life, using all of your values, your unique strengths, and your priorities in ways that add ultimate value to yourself and to the world. This must be crafted without today's limits. You must empower yourself while crafting this vision to remove all of your current limits and image what an abundant future could look like in a perfect world without the possibility of failure or limitation.

ABUNDANCE STATE

If you are going to make lasting change in your life and accomplish something big, you must first master your mindset, or state. Either you control it, or it controls you. The choice is yours.

The Abundance State is simply choosing to operate with the belief that resources are never limited in your life, only resourcefulness is. This requires you see the world in a way that you may not be accustomed to.

Most people, without even realizing it, view the world through the lens of scarcity. They believe resources are limited and that they aren't qualified to receive the abundant riches available to them. They believe these are reserved for the lucky few or the 1 percent we hear so much about in our politics.

Shows like *60 Minutes* or anything on Fox News, CNN, MSNBC, or any other news network that earns revenue through advertising dollars perpetuate the scarcity world view. They paint the world as different than it truly is, as scary, divided, on the verge of collapse. They do this because it's what people pay attention to, not because it's the truth.

Scarcity thinking is predicated on the theory that there's only so much pie to be had. So people will constantly fixate on their own little share of it, rather than understanding they have the ability to grow the pie (abundance). It is a dangerous and contagious way to think, and you must avoid it at all costs.

Once you begin to see things from an Abundance State, your evolution can take hold. The two are entangled and interdependent.

Let's talk more about this.

When you operate from a state of abundance, you can free yourself from the constraints of your fear and the limiting beliefs and emotions that it triggers. Remember, resources are never scarce in today's world, only resourcefulness is.

The Abundance State is driven by empowering beliefs and emotions. Your success, happiness, and fulfillment will grow from its cultivated field.

I use the word *cultivated* because, in the same way a crop thrives by first planting the seed, watering, and fertilizing to encourage growth, and consistently removing weeds and pests to ensure sustainability, you will flourish by:

Deciding you want to be better tomorrow than you are today (planting the seed).

Committing to taking full responsibility for accomplishing this by answering the Six Fundamental Questions.

Practicing for Mastery with AVID (coming later) and by engaging in communities of like-minded people, where you'll build a network of friends, collaborators, and influencers all dedicated to designing radical futures (weed/pest control to ensure sustainability).

Whether you are currently at the top of your game, achieving amazing results in life and business, or struggling with anger, frustration, depression, negativity, or want, changing your thinking in this way is an absolute game-changer.

This may sound like a big claim, and you may be skeptical. But I challenge you to try for yourself and see the results. I have seen a simple shift in thinking and perception radically alter many people's lives for the better. If you're already achieving great success, it will push you beyond your current boundaries into the rarified air that only a tiny percentage of the population breathe. If you're not there yet, you will certainly be well on your way.

MY CALL TO ACTION

"I am born. Whether I shall turn out to be the hero of my own life, or whether that station will be held by anybody else, these pages must show."

—CHARLES DICKENS, *DAVID COPPERFIELD*

Many stories of triumph emerge from the hero's darkest hours. We all know this. What most of us fail to recognize however, is that these tales are not simply fiction, but rather they mirror the events of our own lives. We cycle through countless journeys, playing many different roles, all of which mark us as either conqueror or coward. That is, if we're brave enough to answer the call. The saddest fact of life is that the vast majority of people never actually embark on these paths of evolution. They fail to answer the call to action, to cross the threshold. Thus, they fail to emerge with the treasure of a new life.

Among the ancient live oaks lies Johnson Square, the oldest in the city of Savannah, Georgia. Nestled beneath the gnarly limbs you'll find two fountains, a marble and bronze sundial, and a large obelisk dedicated to Brigadier General Nathanael Greene, a revolutionary war hero. On January 15, 2014, I sat on a bench there and considered my fate.

It was two o'clock in the afternoon, and the light took on a near surreal effect as the grey clouds overhead cast a shadow over the sundial. Permeating the background was the sound of Marion Mays, a local vagabond flautist playing his same old tunes, as if it were just another day. For me, it wasn't.

The coffee in my left hand was getting cold, while I stared through tear-filled eyes at the e-mail on the phone in my right hand. I thought, *This can't be happening to me. I'm only thirty-seven, and my twin boys are five. How can this be the story of my life?*

About a week before, life had been normal. I was happy, healthy, and had no symptoms that suggested concern. One morning I woke up with severe abdominal pain. On my way to work, I stopped at the walk-in clinic across the street, where the attendant doctor recommended a CAT scan to rule out a hernia that might require emergency treatment.

Later that day, the results showed multiple nodules throughout my abdomen extending into the chest, but this is where the scan cut off. So I returned the next day to complete the picture.

On the way back to work, the results, along with the radiologist's opinion, arrived via e-mail. The report referenced "innumerable non-calcified nodules" throughout my abdomen, chest, lungs, and spleen, then the three words that changed my life: "Primary Diagnosis Lymphoma." As I type this today, over two years later, the hair on my arms is standing on end.

I had no idea how advanced the lymphoma was or what course of treatment would be required. I had no idea of my prognosis, and the earliest appointment to see an oncologist was in a month. While I waited, I cycled through emotions and stages of grief. I didn't recognize at the time that this was actually part of my very own hero's journey.

A commonly unconsidered fact is that, if you are suspected of having cancer or any other major illness, the wait to see a specialist can take weeks. During that time for me, I was stewing and imagining cancer cells spreading through my body while analyzing every ache and pain. Waiting and wondering. Over the next few weeks, my wife Melissa and I binge watched our way through Netflix to eat up the hours of the night in an attempt to take our minds off of what was, for us, a desperate and pivotal time. Otherwise, we lived a normal life. Taking care of our boys, dropping them at preschool, going to work, cleaning the house. All the mundane things that are done every day, while this black cloud hung over our heads.

A month later, we pulled into the parking lot of the cancer center at the local hospital. This was a sobering and bewildering experience. We waited for nearly two hours before we were called back. After another thirty-minute wait, the oncologist walked in the room. He came right up to me and looked me in the eyes. He took a long deep breath and exhaled in a sigh that felt like an attempt at empathy. The anxious ball of heat can still be felt, rising in my stomach as I recall this. Then he spoke. I was not prepared for what he said. "I'm sorry. I'm sorry for the confusion. I read your scan and I don't think you have cancer. I think you have sarcoidosis."

Now I didn't know what sarcoidosis was at the time, but it wasn't cancer so it felt like good news. After weeks of believing I was facing a fight for my life, this sent me into a state of shock— and relief.

The doctor walked me across the hallway to meet his friend, the pulmonologist, who explained that sarcoidosis could mimic lymphoma on a scan, but is usually an innocuous disease for people like me.

Melissa and I left the doctor's office, and she was ecstatic. Her joy should have been infectious, but I was numb. It was such an extreme turn around. For the past month, I had been facing the fact that my twins might grow up without me. Now that it was clear my situation was most likely chronic, but not life threatening, I struggled with deciding how to feel about it. Even though I was able to resume my normal life and not have to battle cancer, I didn't feel happy about it, and I couldn't figure out why.

I always find that, when you give yourself the space to think and just be, wisdom will come to you. And this is exactly what happened after some time had passed. When I was able to allow the emotions to subside and look back on what had happened, I realized that I wasn't happy about resuming my normal life because my normal life wasn't fulfilling me. I was not living to the extent I wanted to and was capable of. While I always had goals, rarely did I take the necessary action to achieve them. The mediocrity of the past thirty-seven years hit me head on, unapologetically. I was a world-class underachiever. Average would be a stretch.

To complicate matters, soon after discovering I did not have cancer, we learned that my father-in-law, Pat, actually did. He was diagnosed with melanoma out of nowhere. It had gone unnoticed and spread through his lymph nodes and into many vital organs. His doctors gave him one month to live. Extreme shock. We couldn't wrap our heads around how melanoma could progress to that level unnoticed. But it did. In less than the doctors' estimate of a month, the same period of time that I thought I had cancer, before proper treatment could even begin, Pat passed away at the age of sixty-five.

Pat's funeral service was something else. Hundreds of people showed up that we didn't expect. A massive, standing-room-only crowd gathered as the funeral home manager told us he'd never seen a turn out like this in his life.

For the last seven years, we had lived six hundred miles apart. We spoke on the phone every couple of months to catch up with each other, but I hadn't had the opportunity to see his real life and understand the impact he had on people. Melissa, who spoke with him at least weekly, didn't even know the impact and reach he had.

We stood in awe while a community of people approached us over a two-hour period. They all narrated tearful stories of how Pat was of value in their lives. There was the neighbor down the street who said he was like a father to her when she had nobody, even though they were close to the same age. Friends that struggled with alcohol or drugs that Pat took into his home and helped clean up. People who had lost their jobs and Pat helped them get their confidence back and find new opportunities. Story after story kept coming of how Pat was always there with words of encouragement, hours of his time, or whatever else was needed in the moment. Pat was there, and Pat changed lives. A never-ending supply of people, who loved this man and were grateful to him for the selfless care and value he added, shared their expression of love and sadness with us. I don't know how I didn't notice this the entire time I knew Pat.

When the dust settled and we returned home, the scenes from the funeral, of the people that Pat touched, ran through my mind. I was inspired to start living my life in a way that added value to others as much as Pat did. I'm sure it was the effect of the emotional experience I had just gone through, but the time felt right. I drew a line in the sand and, right then, made the conscious decision to change. To stop underachieving. To stop being less than what I had the potential to be. The output I was generating wasn't enough to pull me toward greatness. I wasn't touching lives in any type of meaningful way. Most importantly, the way in which Pat lived his life made me realize that I wasn't seeing the world through the lens of abundance. I was operating with a scarcity mindset. Always worried about my own resources and my own future. Afraid to take risks, to put myself out there and design an amazing life. I knew I needed to something about this.

Thus began a journey of personal transformation. I knew that if I was going to live up to my potential I had to find a way to be a far better version of myself. In the eighteen months that followed, I consumed hundreds of books, attended seminars, joined mastermind groups, hired personal coaches, and took massive action to change my course.

One day I was on a mastermind group call and my friend, Scott Groves, mentioned a book and podcast by Hal Elrod. The book was *The Miracle Morning*. Scott was saying that this was being called one of the most life-changing books ever written. So, of course, I went out and got it immediately.

In this book, Hal writes about how he created a morning routine that focuses on personal growth after he heard this quote by Jim Rohn, "Your level of success will seldom exceed your level of personal development, because success is something you attract by the person you become." Realizing this was fundamentally true, and that he had no time to focus on personal development, he created a morning routine that included all of the rituals performed by the most successful people in the world. And it changed his life.

It made perfect sense to me, and the Miracle Morning became my routine. Essentially this is waking up an hour before the alarm and practicing all of the rituals that the most successful people in the world have endorsed. These include meditation, affirmations, visualizations, exercise, reading, and journaling.

When I tell you this was a game-changer for me, I am understating it. In short order, all of the personal development I was doing began resulting in massive success in my mortgage banking business. I was closing more than ever. My career reached new heights, and a lot of money was rolling in. The mediocre life of the past thirty-seven years felt like the past, and I was living up to my potential. I had an overwhelming feeling of gratitude and excitement inside. Life was great . . . for a little while. But this is not where my hero's journey ends. It's where it begins.

After reaching the point that I had always identified as "success-ful," it rapidly became apparent that I had misdefined success. Let me tell you, nothing creates a crisis of purpose in life like arriving at a destination that you've gone through so much strife and struggle to find, only to realize that you are in fact lost. But this is exactly where I found myself. Lost at the top of the hill I just climbed. With the demands of my newfound "success" came the self-discovery that I couldn't find meaning and purpose in my work. The money was the only reward, and that wasn't enough for me.

I was successful financially but not emotionally fulfilled, and my work started to suffer. I was finding it more and more difficult every day to be fully engaged with my customers, my clients, and my co-workers in the ways that we needed to sustain and grow the relationships. The work I was doing just felt unimportant. By allowing my despondency to prevail, I began to damage professional relationships and lose big accounts. All the money I was making started to dry up, and I felt miserable every day as I was driving to work. It was clear to everyone around me that something was off. Needing to put an end to the downward spiral I was in, I sat down one day with a journal and a pencil. I re-membered a quote from Tony Robbins that went something like, "Living in alignment with your values is the ultimate success." So I wrote the word "values" on top of the page, and listed what I felt my core values to be. Over a couple of months, this journal-ing exercise eventually led me to ask myself the Six Fundamental Questions that I quickly realized were the foundation that a truly fulfilling life is built upon. It can be said these pages are born from torment and lead to transformation. So many of us share this path. So many more remain where they are born.

A year later, I am happier and more fulfilled than ever before. In the relatively short time that I've been practicing the principles and techniques you're about to learn, my entire life has changed. My circle of friends and sphere of influence has grown exponen-tially, and, for the first time ever, I know that unlimited happiness, fulfillment, and abundance are in my life to stay. Or, at least, that

I can recommit to them any time I want by going back to the Personal Evolution Plan. I want you to experience this for yourself. After all, whether you know it yet or not, you are the hero of your own life. You just need to answer the call.

THE PERSONAL EVOLUTION REVOLUTION

"For me, I am driven by two main philosophies: know more today about the world than I knew yesterday and lessen the suffering of others. You'd be surprised how far that gets you."

—NEIL DEGRASSE TYSON

O ur society is in the midst of a quiet revolution. Fringe notions that were once seen as too new age for practicality are being validated by modern psychology, neuroscience, and even particle physics. These concepts and practices are being utilized by a new generation of leaders and influencers to create new mindsets, new businesses, and new solutions to individual, community, and global problems.

Science is now verifying theories and suppositions that revolutionaries have been using throughout history to achieve high levels of success and in many cases to create evolutions of their own.

Some of the most impactful work in this space includes Positive Psychology (Dr. Martin Seligman), emotional intelligence (Dr. Daniel Goleman), Appreciative Inquiry (Dr. David Cooperrider), and AVID (Dr. Yours Truly) (P.S. I'm not really a doctor).

The Positive Psychology movement uses the abundance of research that shows that when we're in a positive state of mind, our physiology actually changes. We become healthier, live longer, and enjoy better relationships. What's really interesting is that when we approach a problem from a perspective of strength and positivity, the solution centers in our brains come alive and open us up to new, innovative possibilities. It allows us to actually generate new knowledge, as opposed to traditional problem analysis, where we approach a problem from a state of deficit by asking what's broken and how do we fix it? This approach will never yield radical results, but will at best return what's broken to the neutral state of "fixed."

It's important to note that Positive Psychology is not a methodology used by a hippie wearing rose-colored glasses, but is derived from a significant amount of research in neuroscience. The research shows us that, when we are in a negative state, the parts of our brains that are used for solving problems literally close down. Even our physical vision is limited. We actually lose peripheral vision capacity when we operate from a negative state of mind. But when we are positive and optimistic, our brains are ready to imagine any possibility and our vision expands to near 180 degrees. For more on this subject, you can visit the website for the Positive Psychology Center where Dr. Seligman is director.[1]

Appreciative Inquiry is where the rubber of Positive Psychology meets the road of life. It's based on the notion that we grow in the direction of that which we study. Appreciative Inquiry works by focusing on our strengths and potential, also known as the "Positive Core," and directing the energy of this Positive Core toward a vision of transformation and sustainable success. Using what we know of how the solution center in our brains come alive

---

[1]   https://www.authentichappiness.sas.upenn.edu

and allow us to see all possibilities, Appreciative Inquiry causes us to ask affirmative questions that, when contemplated, can spark the generation of new knowledge rather than just making a new distinction from existing knowledge. It's a truly generative process that's mind blowing. I see it as the method by which humanity will hasten its evolution.

Asking good questions, framed in positivity and rooted in a position of strength, allows us to see and apply unlimited possibilities that we may otherwise never consider. You may already realize that the Six Fundamental Questions we cover in this book are rooted in Appreciative Inquiry.

Consider the following question as an example, "What might a truly fulfilling life look like?" Attempting to answer this question forces you to think about designing a fulfilling life from the ground up. It allows you to see new potential and possibilities, because you're envisioning something without constraint. Compare that to how you would answer a similar question framed differently, such as "Why am I not fulfilled?" This question is asked from a position of deficit. You automatically start thinking about what's missing rather than what's possible, and your brain shuts down its capacity to generate solutions.

Emotional intelligence is simply being aware of what emotions are driving you and your decisions, as well as what emotions are driving the people around you. Once you have this awareness, you can begin to offer yourself and others what's actually needed based on the current state of mind, rather than sticking to your previously thought out agenda. There's an abundance of research showing that people with high emotional intelligence (EQ) experience greater mental health, job performance, relationships, and happiness.

Additionally, the personal practices of mindfulness and gratitude and, most importantly, our belief systems are being shown scientifically to alter our very reality. Many have known for a long time, but the rest of us can now see the support of objective evidence. If Napoleon Hill were alive today to view the modern scientific community verifying what he undoubtedly knew in Think and Grow Rich back in 1937, he would probably say, "What the hell took you so long?"

While it's encouraging that today's leaders are using these and other confirmed doctrines to envision and become the best versions of themselves, achieve massive personal growth, and add their valuable contribution to the world, we still see the vast majority of people suffering from a lack of happiness and fulfillment, leading Thoreau's "desperately quiet lives," and dying with greatness still within.

While we have the knowledge and capability to do something about it, a multi-year Gallup study shows us that somewhere between 70 percent and 80 percent of people seem to do nothing to overcome these challenges.

I have put forth the argument that you are much closer than you think to dramatically improving your life. Specifically, that you can stop accepting the status quo and design a Personal Evolution by taking the time to answer and understand Six Fundamental Questions and sustain your change using the daily AVID practice.

Answering the questions with care and authenticity provides you with a contextual understanding of what's separating you from the life you want to and deserve. From a life of greatness. Once this self-knowledge is claimed, you will have a major decision to make that will determine the quality of the rest of your life. That question is, "Are you willing to commit to taking the measured, intentional, and essential action that's required to become the person you need to be? The person that's capable of realizing your dreams.

I hope you answered yes, because it is time to stop accepting anything less than greatness and abundance in your life. It is time to decide to leave the unhappy, unfulfilled, and disengaged majority behind.

HOW TO READ THIS BOOK

This book comes with a free companion course at www.personalevolutionplan.com.

There are two components to reading and extracting the most value from this book.

The first is digesting the *information* in the following pages. The second, and most important, is taking *action* through the self-reflection and inquiry outlined in the Personal Evolution Plan at www.personalevolutionplan.com.

The Six Fundamental Questions are inserted throughout the text rather than in their own separate section. I chose to structure the book in this way because I believe it provides the most natural flow for you, the reader, and allows for you to be presented with information that then directly leads to action and reflection.

The *information* component to this book covers a lot relating to your mindset or *state*. The results and outcomes of everything we do are dependent on the state of mind we operate in. Our state largely controls not only our outcomes, but our very reality experience itself. Everything we see, feel, hear, smell, taste, and think is colored by the state we are in at the time. State is everything. It is the beginning and the end of happiness and fulfillment. This book is your guide to cultivating and living in a state that is most hospitable to manifesting greatness in your life. This is the Abundance State.

You can cultivate this state by:

- Understanding how limiting beliefs and emotions are responsible for the global unhappiness and disengagement epidemic and how this relates to you.

- Understanding the role of fear in generating limiting beliefs and emotions and how to use fear to your advantage as a measuring stick.

- Using Radical Visioning to push through fear and replace it with bravery and curiosity.

- Convert limiting beliefs and emotions to empowering beliefs and emotions with a simple mental exercise.

- Understanding the few basic human needs and how emotions work to satisfy them either in a positive or negative way and what this means for you.

- Using neuroscience to rewire your brain with a compulsion for positivity and happiness.

As for The Personal Evolution Plan, this is where you'll actively design your Radical Vision for the future by taking a deep dive into the Six Fundamental Questions to ignite your Personal Evolution.

1. What are my core values (and why)?
2. What are my unique strengths?
3. What are my top priorities or motivations?
4. What might a radical vision of a truly fulfilling life look like?
5. Why would my radical vision look like that?
6. How might I go about designing my radical, fulfilling life?

The answers to these questions make up your Positive Core and are the foundation for the design of your personal evolution. They will allow you to create a Radical Vision for the future that is in perfect alignment with who you actually are and who you want to become. The answers to these questions represent the best in you. The best of what has been and the best of what will be.

You will then go through the process of following your vision by taking the measured, essential, and intentional action in alignment with your Positive Core. I want to make a distinction here, that it's important to see your vision as a guiding star rather than a distant shore. As psychologist Carl Rogers says, "The good life is a process, not a state of being. It's a direction, not a destination."

The distinction of a guiding star, not a distant shore comes from the work of American and Israeli teacher and writer, Tal Ben-Shahar. You see, when you envision your ideals as a distant shore, you believe that some day you will reach that shore. The problem with this is that when you set your destination too early in your growth process it can create anxiety and stress around your day-to-day activities. This is why most people fail. They stress about what's taking so long to reach the destination or how difficult it will be to navigate the path. But when your vision and ideals are a guiding star, there's no expectation that you'll actually arrive. It's simply a tool to navigate by. This removes all of the stress and anxiety associated with attempting to reach massive life transformative goals. The only thing you need to do is move in the direction of your guiding star (your radical vision) using your Positive Core as your vessel. Now push off and enjoy the adventure. Don't worry about where exactly you'll make landfall. You'll end up exactly where you're supposed to be. Your evolution comes from navigating this course.

Speaking of courses, active, sincere engagement in the Personal Evolution Plan online is the key. If you haven't already, go to www.personalevolutionplan.com and register for the free course.

The Personal Evolution Plan allows you to be more than just a reader. It gives you valuable tools to use this book as a true *choose your own adventure* guide to life.

I also invite you to join a truly special community. The Personal Evolution Tribe is a private and exclusive group of individuals, thought-leaders, and influencers on the path to radically transformative futures. In this community, you can share ideas and goals, give and receive support, and gain accountability through publicly stating your commitments, working with an accountability partner, and collaborating directly with me. I drop in daily to offer coaching and support. I also personally use this community to make sure I'm surrounding myself with people who can add value to my journey and to whom I can add value.

I'm looking forward to getting to know you in The Personal Evolution Tribe and supporting you on your journey from unfulfilled to unlimited! Request to join now! https://www.facebook.com/groups/personalevolutiontribe/

EVOLUTIONARY TRUTHS

FOUNDATIONAL PRINCIPALS

"When I was a child my mother said to me, 'If you become a soldier, you'll be a general. If you become a monk, you'll be the pope.' Instead I became a painter and wound up as Picasso."

—PABLO PICASSO

Social constructionism — The language we use and the ways in which we communicate, both with others and with ourselves, create our reality.

Poetic principal — What we can be in the future largely depends on what we are in the present. Many people feel stuck because of their pasts. The poetic principal gives us license to rewrite, reframe, refocus, and reimagine our past to tell ourselves a new story, to decide a different meaning, and to enable progress toward positive change.

Anticipatory principal — Our visions of the future direct our behavior today. What we expect, we will become.

Positive principal — Positive emotions are shown through research to make you live longer, make more friends, have a happier marriage or relationship, make more money, and have better health. Studies have found that positive emotions actually *produce* success and health just as much as they *reflect* them.

Simultaneity principal — Questions are fateful. Inquiry and change happen in the same moment.

Knowledge is useless if not put to use. Inspiration garners commitment, tactics garner action. You have to start with inspiration, and then get tactical and specific. Most importantly . . . ACT every day.

Achievement begins with visualization. You must be able to visualize the things you want to accomplish before you can accomplish them. You must be able to define and visualize the goal, as well as define the vital functions and vital priorities necessary to accomplish the goal. Otherwise, you will fail.

REMEMBER THE THREE D'S: DISCOVERY, DISTINCTION, DISCIPLINE

When you're consuming information, you are always doing one of these three D's in your mind. You may be *discovering* it for the first time. If so, you may choose to build a new *discipline* around it, or you may do nothing.

If you've heard or seen the information before, it's important not to mentally check out because you already know about it. Rather, try to draw some new *distinction* to understand it differently. This may lead to an epiphany. It's the distinctions, the hearing it a new way, that may move you to create a *discipline* around it. Remember, big doors swing on small hinges. The goal is to create new disciplines around useful concepts.

NOW IS THE TIME TO LEAVE THE UNHAPPY, UNFULFILLED, AND DISENGAGED MAJORITY BEHIND

"The number one cause of mediocrity is never deciding that now matters more than any other time in your life, because it does."

—HAL ELROD

Today is the most extraordinary day in human history. Not because of an event that's occurred, but because the sheer unlimited potential and opportunity that exists right now has never before existed in history. And if you think today is extraordinary, just wait until tomorrow.

The world we live in has shrunk, because of technology and social reach, to such an extent that we now have the ability to bring a concept to reality faster than ever before. Every day, we develop better tools that allow us to share and absorb knowledge, building new platforms to take essential actions that affect massive global change.

We live in an era where we are no longer forced to rely on governments or large corporations to solve humanity's problems. We now have the tools to solve them ourselves, by learning anything we want for free online and using crowdsourcing to gather the people and capital required to affect massive change. Our global intelligence is expanding exponentially through our technology. Over the next twenty years, billions of people will obtain access to electricity and the Internet. Imagine what these newly engaged and empowered people will do, want, and need.

A great example of this is when Peter Diamandis created the X-Prize. He offered a $10,000,000 prize to the team that could launch a reusable manned spacecraft into space twice within two weeks. That one $10,000,000 prize spurred over $400,000,000 in investments into the endeavor and has launched a completely new industry, with great people like Elon Musk and Jeff Bezos competing for supremacy, accelerating advancement, and taking us where we have never been before on multiple fronts.

I mention this because I want to urge you to think big when you think of your future. Make your future radical! Everybody told Peter there was no way he could accomplish his mission of creating a space tourism industry, but he pressed forward and leveraged human potential in a truly creative way, and he is succeeding. Peter has since moved on the even bigger "moonshot" projects with his company, Human Longevity, Inc., where he's teamed up with the brightest minds in genomics, stem cell research, and human health to achieve the goal of extending human life by fifty-plus years immediately, and eventually allow us to live virtually indefinite lifespans. Talk about radical!

Be like Peter! Now is the time to imagine a radical future where you not only create a life of prosperity and enrichment for yourself, but you also have the largest impact you can on the people around you. It's time to be audacious in your self-image and decide to change the world by changing yourself and what you believe you're capable of.

Contrary to what the twenty-four-hour news cycle will have you believe, crime, hunger, poverty, murder, disease, complications of birth, war, violence, racism, sexism, discrimination, and inequality are at all-time lows in recorded history.[2] All this while life expectancy, charitable giving, cutting-edge research, access to information, global employment, and altruism are at all-time highs. There are more millionaires and billionaires in the world now that at any other time, and it's easier to join their ranks than ever before.

The potential and opportunity for unlimited happiness and fulfillment exists everywhere. But it begins within us and is only realized externally through mastery of ourselves and our surroundings and purposeful action. Before you can achieve greatness, you must first know what you want, why you want it, and, most importantly, become a person with the ability to handle it.

Have you ever wondered why so many people are unhappy and unfulfilled even though we're living through such an extraordinary time of potential and opportunity? I believe it's because we don't dream anymore, and we certainly don't see ourselves as the heroes of our own lives. We don't feel it's appropriate to have a Radical Vision of the future.

We're compelled by the people in our lives and the institutions we've created to conform, to be like each other rather than to be radical; to be calm and keep our mouths shut rather than to be excited and speak with passion; to think small and not to dream

---

[2] http://thinkprogress.org/security/2013/12/11/3036671/2013-certainly-year-human-history/

big; to wait for our circumstances to change before we act out the best versions of ourselves. This never happens.

We learn to see our dreams as delusions of grandeur. We dismiss them as unrealistic, beyond our scope, and even irresponsible, when the fact is, the only thing that's unrealistic and irresponsible is settling for less than what we can be. When we do that, the only thing that's beyond our scope is a happy and fulfilled life.

Conventional wisdom can never change the world, and that my friend is exactly what we need to do. It begins within each of us, and then extends out of us through our personal circles, into our communities, and across the globe. By engaging in personal evolutionary behavior, we form a catalyst for collective change.

Gallup has been tracking engagement and happiness since 1997. What they've learned from the millions of surveys that have been returned—yes, millions of surveys, tracked for the past nineteen years—is that, consistently, over 70 percent of people are disengaged, unhappy, and unfulfilled at work.

This is not just a work problem. The unhappiness and disengagement extend to our personal lives as well.

This fact not only takes a massive emotional toll on people, it is also shown to be costing us somewhere between $450 to $550 billion per year in lost productivity, just in the United States. If this has such a massive economic impact, just imagine the impact it has on our health and well-being and the health and well-being of our families and friends, who are the innocent victims of our fulfillment void.

I believe our refusal to dream big, our unhappiness, dissatisfaction, and disengagement stem from one primary cause: FEAR.

Our fears trigger limiting beliefs and limiting emotions. For example, think of something big that you want to accomplish in life. I'll bet there are a bunch of fears surrounding it. The fear of failure, fear of rejection, fear of looking foolish, fear of embarrassing yourself, fear of not being validated, or fear of losing time or money.

These fears embody themselves as limiting beliefs. Limiting beliefs like:

"I'm not good enough; I don't deserve it; I don't know enough; I don't have enough experience; I don't have enough time; I don't have enough money; I don't know the right people; I'm too old; I'm too young; I'm too fat; I'm too ugly; I don't have the prerequisites."

Of course it's easy to see these limiting beliefs as negative, but in actuality they are like pain pills. They shield us from having to directly face the fear that drives us. They are the excuses we make that allow us to avoid facing our fears and doing the things that scare us. They hedge against the risk of failure, rejection, embarrassment, non-validation, loss, and whatever other fears exist within us, and this makes us feel good. It makes us feel safe.

We trade our happiness and fulfillment for this safety. We do this to our great detriment. We do this at the expense of our fulfillment. We withhold our value from the world, and the world suffers.

The crazy thing is, there's no reason to do this. The things we are afraid of are never as bad as we imagine them to be.

For example, think of a time when the worst happened. When something you were afraid of actually happened to you. Maybe you put yourself out there, and it didn't work out. Maybe someone took advantage of you or hurt you by not validating or accepting you. Maybe you felt hurt and embarrassed. What happened to your fear in this moment? Really try to put yourself there. What was your state of mind when the thing that you feared became your reality? I'm willing to bet that your fear was gone. It was replaced with whatever emotion you were feeling at the time.

I'll bet that emotion began as anger, sadness, embarrassment, frustration, anxiety, or even hatred, but after time morphed into a feeling of resilience and determination. Determination not to let it keep you down. You weren't afraid anymore. You were empowered, because you no longer saw your happiness and fulfillment through the lens of outward acceptance. When your fear became your reality, you gained perspective, strength, and determination. Think about some times in your life when this has happened.

The point of this thought exercise is to prove that, even if your fears become your reality, you cannot fail. Your worst-case scenario is that you will empower yourself and rid yourself of the need for external validation.

When we refuse to trade our happiness and fulfillment for safety and make the conscious decision to replace our fear with bravery and curiosity, we will convert our limiting beliefs to empowering beliefs.

The best way to do this is to ask yourself the right questions. To start, ask yourself, "What *must* I believe to achieve a radical future? What *must* I believe to (fill in the blank with anything you want)?"

The answer is simple. You *have* to believe:

"I *am* good enough; I *do* deserve it; I *do* know enough; I *do* have enough experience; I'll find the time; I am enough; I will not fail."

These empowering beliefs are the wings that propel you to a higher level of happiness, fulfillment, and engagement. To a higher state.

When you commit to a Radical Vision for your future, you are inherently forced to hold these empowering beliefs as truths. When you're empowered, you'll realize that you don't have to be everything all at once, you just have to be authentic. When you're authentic, the vast majority of people will like and appreciate you, and, more importantly, being authentic means you're acting in alignment with your values. Doing this means you can never fail. You can only learn, grow, and reiterate.

—2—

GREATNESS DEMANDS POSITIVITY

"Curating a state of love, gratitude, contribution, determination, and abundance in your mind is the foundation for a life of unlimited happiness and fulfillment."

—MIKE MERRIAM

There are some people who live with a mastery of life. In other words, they are happy and fulfilled, constantly striving to be better tomorrow than they are today. I know many of these people. They are friends, mentors, and coaches. They are the people I've chosen to surround myself with, because I know that they'll rub off on me. I've chosen to surround myself with these people and to actively curate my interactions because I know that emotions are contagious. The right people and groups will elevate me to a higher level and keep me working toward a mastery of life.

Who do you surround yourself with? As the great Jim Rohn said, "You are the average of the five people you spend the most time with."

So who's in your top five?

Two years ago, my top five needed some serious upgrading. I actively worked on adding people to my sphere (or finding a way into theirs) that were already in places that I wanted to be. This act alone has had the largest impact on my life. The people we surround ourselves and interact with hold a massive amount of power over our lives. Choose them wisely if you wish to master life.

To live with a mastery of life, we must first learn to master our emotions.

Many of us allow our emotions to control our state of mind rather that our state of mind controlling our emotions. We forgot who's boss. We forgot how to choose. We're so overloaded with noise that we just sit back and accept the emotions manifested by our experiences and make no significant effort to rid ourselves of the ones that do us harm—our limiting emotions. How many times do you hear people say, "That's life," and accept mediocrity or some other stifling circumstance? How often are you guilty of this? Of "I can't" syndrome?

Limiting emotions are the ones we associate with negativity or bad feelings. Things like anxiety, anger, jealousy, fear, depression, frustration, hatred, and so on.

Limiting emotions cause us to take actions, or worse, not take actions that ensure our basic human emotional needs aren't satisfied. For example, the vast majority of people allow fear of failure to prevent them from trying something bold. When in fact, the very act of trying, whether successful or not, causes significant growth.

When our needs aren't satisfied, we experience even more limiting emotions. The cycle not only continues, it intensifies until it reaches a tipping point where we begin to cause damage to our lives. Some turn to alcohol or drugs, some to unhealthy food or relationships. There are unlimited ways in which we can fill the voids caused by unmet needs. None of them are good for us.

So what are the basic human emotional needs? Unlike emotions, which number in the thousands, although we tend to only recognize a few, there are only a handful of human needs.

You may be familiar with Maslow's hierarchy of needs. Maybe you've heard anecdotal talk about it. Many people misunderstand what Maslow's work was all about.

Abraham Maslow specified a psychological theory in his 1954 work, "Motivation and Personality," in which he outlined five basic human needs. The needs were:

1. Physiological (survival)
2. Safety (certainty)
3. Love & Belonging (connection)
4. Esteem (significance)
5. Self-Actualization (growth)

In later years, Maslow realized there was one big thing missing from his list. A sixth need. He called this self-transcendence. He stated, "The self only finds its actualization in giving itself to some higher goal, in altruism and spirituality." I prefer the more simplified concept of contribution as the sixth human need.

Many others have gone on to study the field of universal human needs, and research supports their existence and validity. Although there are some conflicting opinions over the order of needs and the differences caused by age and culture. I don't believe these differences are important. What is important to understand is that there are foundational needs and elevating needs.

The foundational needs are the first four:

1. Survival
2. Certainty
3. Connection
4. Significance

For our purposes, we can drop survival from our list and assume that if you're reading this book, you have access to food, water, shelter, and the other basic necessities of life.

Additionally, I want to point out that certainty only represents one side of a coin. The other side of the certainty coin is hope. Hope will replace survival as our fourth foundational need. This updated list is explained below:

THE FOUNDATIONAL NEEDS

Certainty - We all need a level of certainty in our lives. We want to know that we are safe and comfortable and that the things we depend on for our quality of life—such as our jobs, our income, our family and friends—are safe and secure. Simultaneously, however, we can't have too much certainty or we'll be bored. We need the hope that we can improve our lives.

Hope - If everything in our lives were 100 percent certain, there would be no hope for a brighter future. If everything in our lives remained unchanged, it would be dull and boring, eventually depressing. Living with complete certainty would be a terrible way to live. Uncertainty gives us hope. Hope that we can build a better life, overcome a hardship, and remain open to new possibilities. After all, if I had to issue a primary directive for the human race, it would be for us all to be a little better tomorrow than we are today.

Connection - This is straightforward. We need to be connected to others through society, family, friendships, and intimate relationships. The strongest form of connection is love.

Significance - Ah, significance. Our need to actually matter, to be relevant and needed, to be here for a reason. So many of us are driven by this need. This can be both the greatest and the most dangerous of the basic human needs, depending on the actions we take to satisfy it. More on this statement in a minute.

These four needs are our foundational needs. These are the things that all of us must, and will, satisfy regardless of what else we do in life. We satisfy these foundational needs in two ways, with positive actions and with negative actions. Tony Robbins gives the following as anecdotal examples when he talks about the basic human needs.

Consider Osama Bin Laden. It's fair to say he was driven by a need to be *significant*. He was one of twenty-some children in his family. It would not be a stretch to say that he felt insignificant. The actions he took to satisfy this need were to commit acts of terrorism and kill innocent people. Instant significance.

Now take the case of Mother Teresa. It may not be apparent, but Mother Teresa valued significance as well. But how did Mother Teresa go about being significant? She understood that true significance is in being of service to others, through *contribution*. She dedicated her life to serving those people in the world who were in the most desperate need of help. The people that nobody else would serve.

These examples show two people taking vastly different actions to satisfy the same basic need. Who do you think was happier? More fulfilled? Who had a better impact on others?

Clearly these questions are ridiculous to even contemplate because the answers are so obvious. This is the clarity of mind you must develop in understanding all of the actions you take to satisfy your foundational needs. This type of clarity comes from under-standing your values, strengths, and priorities—your Positive Core.

This is an extreme example but it's relevant to all of us. We all act in ways that are either positive or negative in order to meet the foundational needs that drive us. Negativity in all its incarnations, is always limiting. This is why Positive Psychology is fundamental to growth.

Neuroscience research on Positive Psychology shows that when we approach a problem with a negative mindset, the part of our brains responsible for creating solutions literally closes off. The mental resources available to us become extremely limited.

Conversely, when we approach a problem with a positive mind-set, rooted in bravery and curiosity, we open ourselves up to unlim-ited opportunity. When we ask ourselves how we can model what's already great and create even more greatness around us, our brains are open to literally unlimited possibilities. This subtle difference in approach leads to staggering differences in outcomes.

To illustrate this, consider that some of the largest, most well-known businesses, governments, and even the United Nations and the Dali Lama are using this concept in a practice known as Appre-ciative Inquiry (AI). This process is resulting in some of the greatest achievements in business, in governance, and in humanity today. In a 2004 United Nations report issued by Secretary General Kofi Annan, Appreciative Inquiry was described as "the best large-group planning methodology in the world today."

A great example of AI at work is the Sustainable Cleveland 2019 initiative, which I have had the great honor of personally co-facilitating with the Flourishing Leadership Institute.

Mayor Frank Jackson is passionate and dedicated to the city of Cleveland, Ohio, becoming a global leader in sustainability. When he declared "The time is now for Cleveland, and I refuse to miss this opportunity" and approached Dr. David Cooperrider, creator of Appreciative Inquiry, to help co-design and lead an unprecedented sustainability summit using AI, Cleveland forever changed and is now on the path to becoming a "Green City on a Blue Lake."

At this summit, an idea was generated to create a wind farm on Lake Erie to provide sustainable energy to the city of Cleveland. This idea represents a radical vision for Cleveland's future. Unleashing the Positive Core of the city and directing its energy toward this Radical Vision has resulted in the city of Cleveland being awarded a grant for $40 million dollars from the U.S. Department of Energy, in May of 2016, to build the world's first ever-fresh water wind farm.

This is just one example that I have personal experience with where the Appreciative Inquiry approach is creating radical change across human systems. There are many more examples of this. For more information, you can visit www.evolve2flourish.com.

The reason AI is so effective, is because it asks the right questions. Questions rooted in the affirmative and the positive. Traditional problem analysis is rooted in deficit. The deficit is the question "What's broken and how do we fix it?" This question starts the brain off in a negative state, and, as we've discussed, this limits the solutions we are capable of creating. We will never achieve a great solution using this approach. The best we can hope to achieve is the neutral position of taking what's broken and returning it to functional. We certainly will not take what's broken and make it world-class.

The questions we must ask are: "Where are we already great?" "What worked in other areas or in the past?" "What works on a world-class level?" "What might it look like if we achieved excellence?"

These questions open up our brains to unlimited resources by engaging our imaginations to create new solutions without being limited by today's constraints.

These principles apply across all scales, from businesses, to governments, to communities, and all the way down to the individual.

Take a step back and analyze your behavior and the behavior of your friends and family. Do you see where you may be operating from a state of deficit and how it's preventing you from seeing the big picture and making the changes in your life that you desire? Really stop and think about this. Where can you use the principals of Appreciative Inquiry to open yourself up to unlimited opportunity?

As we progress through this book, it's important to remember that everything we do is rooted in the satisfaction of our four foundational needs, which are:

1. Certainty
2. Hope
3. Connection
4. Significance

We're going to learn to take only positive action to satisfy our foundational needs, which then brings into focus our elevating needs.

Our elevating needs are *growth* and *contribution*. These are the parents of the Abundance State and the brush and canvas of your Personal Evolution.

Let's examine these:

Growth - Personal growth is an elevating need because, when we become better versions of ourselves, we give ourselves the greatest gift imaginable—the ability to take what we've learned and teach it to others. Through growth, we're able to put our world into perspective and gain the clarity of desires and emotional mastery we need to lead an evolved life.

Contribution - It is through our contribution to others and to the world that we live with purpose. This is where real *certainty, hope, significance, connection, happiness,* and *fulfillment* come from. Contribution, my friends, is the secret to life. Remember this. The key to life is contribution.

This brings us to our first Fundamental Question.

—3—

FUNDAMENTAL QUESTION #1

WHAT ARE MY CORE VALUES (AND WHY)?

"It's not hard to make decisions when you know what your values are."
—ROY DISNEY

Values are a common concept, but, when pressed, most people struggle articulating exactly what are the core values that drive them. Can you immediately list your Core Values? You'll want to put some thought into this, because you're about to be asked to do so.

Your Core Values are the heart of your Positive Core and should inform every decision you make in pursuit of your Radical Vision.

In other words, your values define your value to the world. Finding a way to deploy your value in the world, while creating shared prosperity for yourself and the people you impact, is the ultimate success.

In fact, the highest use of Radical Visioning is for you to create prosperity in the world by envisioning and becoming the best possible version of yourself through measured, intentional, and essential action in alignment with your values, strengths, and priorities, to create marketable solutions that fulfill community or global needs.

It's important to understand how your values relate to your foundational needs. Remember, there are six basic human needs—four foundational needs and two elevating needs. The foundational needs will always be satisfied, either through positive or negative behaviors and actions. If you recall, these four primary needs are

1. Certainty
2. Hope
3. Connection
4. Significance

It is only when we can satisfy our foundational needs with positive behaviors and actions and live mindfully with essential focus on what truly matters, that we can focus on our elevating needs of *growth* and *contribution.*

Unlike the foundational needs, elevating needs are not possible to satisfy with negative behaviors and actions. They do not have a negative form. They only exist as benevolent concepts. In other words, growth and contribution are inherently positive. Thus, when we pursue our foundational needs with positive behaviors and actions, we pivot to a state where we have the potential to make our greatest contribution to others and to the world. This potential is realized when we place essential focus on growth and contribution.

It is through our personal growth that we are able to make our greatest contribution. The greater our contribution, the more certainty, hope, connection, and significance we build. Can you see how this cycle works? It's an ever-improving mechanism. This is the definition of evolution.

You should have already accomplished your first call to action, registering for the Personal Evolution Plan. If you did not, you should do so now.

CALL TO ACTION

Go to WWW.PERSONALEVOLUTIONPLAN.COM and complete MODULE 1: Core Values.

WELCOME BACK FROM THE WEB!

We just took a deep dive into identifying your Core Values. You were asked to answer a series of questions related to exploring your identity, your character, and your ethics which should have led you to create a list of at least five core values.

How hard was it to think of your five most important values? For some people this is a very difficult exercise, for others it's easy. Regardless, it makes us think. The first time I did this, I have to admit I was a little stumped at first and found it difficult to come up with five.

Now that you know your top five values, it's important to be honest with yourself when considering if your actions are always in alignment. Chances are, there are many times when your actions do not align with your values.

When you engage in gossip or talk behind a friend or family member's back, which many, if not all of us have been guilty of at some point, you are not being true to your values. If your values include jealousy and duplicity, then perhaps you are being true to them with these actions, but I sincerely doubt these are on your list.

Making sure your actions and decisions are always aligned with the values you've identified is instrumental in making progress toward the Abundance State. This is why we did the 5 Why's exercise. I strongly urge you to take the time to do the 5 Why's with each one of your values, unique strengths, and priorities. This will give you the deep contextual perspective that you need to be the embodiment of your ideals.

The 5 Why's was developed by Sakichi Toyoda and used in the Toyota Motor company to evolve their manufacturing methodologies. It is an iterative process that has us ask "why" five times. Doing this reveals the true nature of a problem as well as its solution. When we apply it to beliefs, such as our values, it can have a powerful effect on how we actually align our actions in congruence with our beliefs.

Here's an example based on my honesty value.

WHY IS HONESTY IMPORTANT TO ME?

Because I believe people deserve the truth.

WHY DO PEOPLE DESERVE THE TRUTH?

Because I believe that falsehoods can hurt them.

WHY CAN FALSEHOODS HURT THEM?

Because I believe falsehoods can trigger improper actions.

WHY CAN FALSEHOODS TRIGGER IMPROPER ACTIONS?

Because I believe if a person operates with falsehoods, they don't have the proper context to make good decisions.

WHY IS A PERSON HAVING THE PROPER CONTEXT TO MAKE GOOD DECISIONS IMPORTANT?

Because I believe that when people make good decisions, their lives and the lives of everyone they are connected to improve.

So . . . analyzing all of this, go back to the first question and look at the last answer.

WHY IS HONESTY IMPORTANT TO ME?

Because it improves people's lives.

If I was to make the statement that one of my values is honesty, it really doesn't come with much meaning or significance. Sure, it feels right to say that honesty is a value but it's more important to understand *why* honesty is a value. This way, when I'm going about my life, my honesty value carries significantly more meaning for me, and I'm much less apt to take action that misaligns with this value.

A couple months ago, I was having breakfast on the roof of a hotel in San Diego where I had just finished a three-day mastermind meeting. I got off the elevator and walked out to the rooftop lounge where my buddy Scott Groves was sitting there with his wife and newborn baby. With them was a guy named Josh that I hadn't met before. They asked me to join them.

Josh asked me about what I was doing and I told him about this book. The 5 Why's came up and he asked me to run him through it. I agreed and asked him to name one of his Core Values. He answered, "Expression."

Then I asked why expression was important and he stated that because expressing himself fully helped him avoid the pain that comes from not doing so. I continued on with asking why, each time rephrasing the question in accordance with his answer. For example, "why is avoiding this pain important?" By the fourth why, he had stated, "Because expression is the meaning of life."

Well, I don't know about you, but I thought this was the perfect iteration of this exercise. How much more weight do you think Josh's expression value has for him when making decisions in his life now? He went from using expression to avoid pain to having his expression value become the actual meaning of life. This is the power of the 5 Why's exercise.

Using the 5 Why's process in each section of your Personal Evolution Plan is a great tool for taking a deep dive into what really drives you and developing a clear contextual understanding of your pathway forward from unfulfilled to unlimited.

There are a few things to keep in mind when using the 5 Why's. It's not a science. It's based on your beliefs and your state of mind while performing the exercise. Repeated attempts at the same questions can yield different results. Also, you may not actually need the full five why's. You may get to a final answer by the third or fourth why. Playing with when to stop and when to keep going can be insightful.

It's an amazing exercise, but you have to remain loose about it. Focus hard on your answers, but hold the results loosely. In other words, be willing to allow your answers to change and to flow. You can apply this exercise to any area of your life at any stage of your life. It will always grow with you.

Now that you've gotten a much deeper and contextual understanding of your Core Values, using mindfulness and essential focus will help you significantly, by driving behaviors that ensure you are satisfying your foundational needs with positive actions.

Commit to being hyper self-aware when analyzing how your actions align with your values. Don't lie to yourself to protect your ego. Chances are, when you completed the Core Value exercises, you found many areas in your life where your actions and values are not in alignment.

You will most likely continue to find these areas. This is okay. It's normal. It's a human condition. When you make the decision to live in a positive, mindful, essentially focused, and determined state, it will very quickly become easier to guarantee you are always acting in alignment with your values. Pretty soon, it will be second nature.

It's also important to understand that your values will change over time. As you grow, your values will morph and grow with you. It is okay to replace one value with another, or even drop one completely if it doesn't fit with the life you desire, at any point in time. This change is healthy and is integral to the growth of the individual.

As Winston Churchill said, "To improve is to change; to perfect is to change often."

CALL TO ACTION

GO TO THE PERSONAL EVOLUTION TRIBE ON FACEBOOK AND POST YOUR CORE VALUES.

SHARE WHAT YOU'VE LEARNED ABOUT YOURSELF USING THE EXERCISES IN STEP 1.

LEAVE FEEDBACK OF SUPPORT ON SOMEONE ELSE'S POST.

Research shows that when we engage, learn, and develop in group environments we do so with an exponential increase in results compared with self-study and reflection. The power of the group is significant. Don't miss out on the opportunity to use it to advance more rapidly on whatever path you are on.

Not only will you benefit from the power of group learning and engagement, you will be taking positive action to satisfy two of your four foundational needs, connection and significance. The group literally exists as a tool for all of us to shorten our path to unlimited happiness and fulfillment.

As John Ratzenberger said, "Find people who share your values, and you'll conquer the world together."

HOW LANGUAGE AND EMOTIONS CREATE REALITY

"What really matters for success, character, happiness, and lifelong achievements is a definite set of emotional skills—your EQ—not just purely cognitive abilities that are measured by conventional IQ tests."

—DANIEL GOLEMAN

Our understanding of emotions is extremely limited by the language we use to describe them. There are thousands of emotions that we feel on a regular basis but don't have the language to properly distinguish. This is why we respond so well to metaphors and memes. They validate what we're feeling but don't necessarily have the ability to verbally articulate.

Positive emotions tend to be much less intense and more difficult to grasp than negative emotions, but they contribute fundamentally to desired life outcomes such as happiness, friendships, marital satisfaction, higher incomes, and better health.3 For this reason, it's paramount to focus on the emotions you feel, and to learn to cultivate desired positive emotions. You'll learn how to do this later on using the AVID process. If you just can't wait, you can always visit the AVID course in Personal Evolution Plan at www. personalevolutionplan.com. If you can wait, please read on.

Think back on all the emotions you've felt over the past couple of weeks. For most of us, the list is equally distributed, with half negative (limiting) emotions and half positive (empowering).

Many of us pass easily through the range of these emotions throughout our lives. On any given day, we may experience varying levels of happiness, sadness, fulfillment, frustration, joy, anger, determination, fear, and so on. Then there are the other times in life when significant events occur that drive the emotions we feel. As with everything, these events either trigger negative, limiting emotions or positive, empowering emotions.

Many believe this is the natural pattern of life. The fact is it can be the natural pattern of life, if we aren't careful to consciously decide otherwise. The problem is most of us don't decide otherwise. We allow the status quo to overtake our lives.

I was having a conversation the other day, and I was pontificating (I'm sure in an annoying way) about how so many people have conversations rooted in negativity and how damaging this is to our culture. I was saying how the conversations we have are of extreme importance. We are actively building the culture we live in, one conversation at a time. The language we use and the framework of our interactions, questions, discussions, and conversations have an enormous impact on the reality of our lives. In essence, the way in which we choose to converse determines our realities.

---

3 http://www.ncbi.nlm.nih.gov/pmc/articles/PMC3156028/pdf nihms304992. pdf

Someone responded to my disdain for negatively framed conversations with the statement, "Well more negative things happen to us in life than positive things. That's why there's a lot of negative conversation."

At first I didn't know how to respond to this. I was caught off guard because I don't see life as more negative than positive and hadn't ever considered this. Frankly, it kind of blew my mind. I responded with something like, "It's all in how we allow the things that happen to affect us," and then the conversation went in a different direction as other people came into the room.

It wasn't until the next day that I got to thinking about this and realized what I should have said. I should have said what's true. And here it is.

There are very few negative things that happen *to* us. Yes, while things do happen *to* us that are the result of bad luck, such as car accidents, disease, losing loved ones, etc., the vast majority of things in life don't happen *to* us, they happen as a result *of* us.

By far, things that happen in our lives that we perceive as negative are due to a previous action that we either took or did not take. Had we taken different actions in the past, most of the negative things that happen in our lives could have been avoided.

We have to be careful about slipping into a victim mentality. We always want to operate from a growth mindset, as opposed to a fixed mindset. A fixed mindset is one that says, "I am who am I am. I have the tools I have and that's that. I have to work with what I've been given." How many times do you hear people say, "I'm just not that kind of person," or "I'm the type of person that (fill in the blank)"? Maybe you've been guilty of saying these phrases. It's easy to slip in to. When I hear this, I always want to ask, "When did the person you are become set in stone? When did you decide that you're done growing?"

The growth mindset, on the other hand, is one that says, "I am not my past. I am not limited by my present abilities, but rather,

I have the ability to learn and the ability to grow. I will be better tomorrow than I am today."

A great psychologist out of Stanford University, Dr. Carol Dweck, directed a study in which children were separated into two groups. They were all given a very easy test and all did quite well on it. One group was told that they did well and they must be smart, while the other group was told that they did well and they must have worked hard.

Then all the children were given a very difficult test, which nobody did well on.

Later, they were brought back and given the same easy test they originally took. What do you think happened?

The group that was told they were smart performed 25 percent worse the second time around, while the group that was told they must have worked hard performed 25 percent better.

Why is this? Because "being smart" is a fixed state while "working hard" is a growth state. When something happens that shakes your confidence—in this case, the difficult test—and you are operating from a fixed state, you will begin to think that you aren't as smart as you thought you were, and your capabilities actually shrink in the face of new challenges.

Dr. Dweck puts it like this, "In a fixed mindset, students believe their basic abilities, their intelligence, their talents are just fixed traits. They have a certain amount and that's that, and then their goal becomes to look smart all the time and never look dumb. In a growth mindset, students understand that their talents and abilities can be developed through effort, good teaching, and persistence. They don't necessarily think everyone's the same or anyone can be Einstein, but they believe everyone can get smarter if they work at it."

The students that operate from the fixed mindset do themselves a tremendous disservice. If their goal is to always look smart and never look dumb, then they will never be able to learn on a high level because they'll be afraid to fail.

When people operate from a fixed mindset, they tend to sit back and wait for good things to happen to them. Rather than understanding what happens is a result of who they are becoming, in other words, a result of their growth or lack thereof. One of the biggest mistakes that people make in life is thinking that happiness will come from a changed circumstance. From an external factor being different or better in their lives.

Let me be clear when I say this. There are no external circumstances in your life that are responsible for your happiness or unhappiness, and there are no external circumstances that you can change that will result in lasting happiness and fulfillment. It seems cliché to say, but most people still think they can be happy if they achieve a goal, or make more money, or get a different job, or move to a different city, or buy a new car.

None of this will make you happy for very long. Not unless you take the time for self-reflection, understand this basic truth, and change your inside world first.

Many people tell themselves that they'll start acting a certain way when they get to a certain place. That when they achieve X they will somehow be a different person and thrive in life. This is an utterly false assumption. If you can't find a way to be happy right now, you will never be happy.

Forgive the platitude, but it seems many people still don't get it. Happiness comes from within you. We've been hearing that for centuries and it still proves true.

Let's talk about where within you it comes from. It is cultivated by replacing limiting beliefs and emotions with empowering beliefs and emotions, and then taking actions in alignment with your Positive Core toward your Radical Vision. It comes from cultivating the right state. All of this culminates as "Living With Purpose." For an example of how to accomplish this, watch the video titled

"Converting Limits to Empowerments" in the Personal Evolution Plan online.

Living with this purpose ensures that your foundational needs are satisfied with positive actions. The progress that is made with these actions is what gives rise to happiness.

That happiness is then fed and sustained by focusing on our elevating needs (*growth* and *contribution*). When we place continued effort on our personal growth, we hone our ability to contribute with great efficacy. When we contribute on a high level, we live with unlimited happiness and fulfillment. We evolve.

In *The 7 Habits of Highly Successful People*, Steven Covey states, "In doing so [achieving personal growth], we counteract entropy—the tendency of all things to eventually break down." He goes on, "The resolve to live by values based on principles is renewed and deepened. Our batteries are recharged. The saw becomes sharper. Your life becomes sharper. You are able to do your work better, faster, wiser. You are able to love unconditionally, to take initiative, to be both courageous and compassionate simultaneously. You're able to sidestep negative energy rather than give away your space to those people or things that seem to control you. When you don't sidestep, you literally give up your freedom to choose your response. You disempower yourself and empower others' weakness to continue to mess up your life. You are not living; you are being lived."

DON'T "BE LIVED." LIVE WITH VIGOR.

—5—

FUNDAMENTAL QUESTION #2

WHAT ARE MY UNIQUE STRENGTHS?

"No one can discover you until you do. Exploit your talents, skills, and strengths and make the world sit up and take notice"
—ROB LIANO

Now that you've done an extensive review of your values and hopefully went through the 5 Why's process with each them, we're going to look at your unique strengths.

Maybe you already know what your strengths are. Maybe you don't think you have any. Trust me, you do. You have an abundance of strength, knowledge, and value to give to others. In this section, we are going to identify what this is and teach you how to deliver your value to the world.

CALL TO ACTION

Go to WWW.PERSONALEVOLUTIONPLAN.COM and complete
MODULE 2: UNIQUE STRENGTHS

WELCOME BACK FROM THE WEB!

In Module 2 of your Personal Evolution Plan, you went through the VIA Character Strengths Survey in order to define your twenty-four signature strengths. These signature strengths are based on the work of Dr. Martin Seligman, who is widely known as the father of Positive Psychology.

Seligman came up with the idea that rather than focusing on being *happy*, we should instead attempt to *flourish*. He created a concept known as PERMA, which stands for Positive emotion, Engagement, Relationships, Meaning, and Achievement. Focusing on these five components is what allows people to flourish, which is far more important and comprehensive than our standard definition of happiness.

Seligman describes virtue as that which underpins PERMA. In his research of all the great texts throughout history, he discovered that there are six overarching virtues that seem to exist in all of them. The six virtues are:

1. Wisdom and Knowledge

2. Courage

3. Humanity

4. Justice

5. Temperance

6. Transcendence

He then took these six virtues and created twenty-four signature strengths out of them. These strengths are instrumental in designing and manifesting your Radical Vision for the future.

In the exercise you just completed, you should have taken the time to answer some important questions designed to trigger your brain to see you from a position of strength. This is the essence of Positive Psychology. By asking questions designed to illicit high-value responses rooted in your self-esteem and memories of being at your best, you are able to clearly define your unique value. The goal is to start thinking about how you can take something that you currently don't like to do, and apply your greatest strength to it.

Here's a recap of the questions we asked:

- What are some challenges I've faced in my life and how did I overcome them?

- What do I like about myself?

- What do people compliment me on?

- What do I enjoy doing?

- What am I proud of?

Now that you know your twenty-four signature strengths, it's important to analyze how often you use these to get what you want out of life. Are you using your strengths to achieve a personal evolution, or are you submitting to the strengths of others while life passes you by?

Do you use your strengths to improve your life at work, or do you just go through the motions and act how you think others want you to act? What are some ways you can use your strengths more often at work?

How about in your relationships? Do you use your strengths to enhance your relationships? What are some ways you can improve your relationships using your unique strengths?

Ask yourself the same question in all of the other key areas of your life, your health, your finances, and your spirituality or passion.

Be mindful and honest with yourself. Self-awareness around when, where, and how you use your unique strengths in alignment with your values is essential on your journey from unfulfilled to unlimited. Be cognizant of this, and find ways to use your strengths in your key areas more often. You'll be amazed at how your life will change.

The best thing about using your strengths is that the more you use them the stronger they become. When they are strengthened to a tipping point, you will spawn the development of new strengths, emerging strengths. The ones that are just below the surface and are there for your use when you push yourself and when you are called upon to persevere. These will open up new opportunities for greatness in your life.

Just remember, stay essentially focused on your values and unique strengths. Decide to live in the Abundance State, take action every day in every key area of life, and you will live with unlimited happiness and fulfillment. You'll be amazed at how the universe aligns to allow you to achieve greatness. I guarantee it!

In case you need it again, here's the link to the VIA Character Strength Survey:

http://personalevolution.pro.viasurvey.org/character-survey

CALL TO ACTION

Go to The Personal Evolution Tribe on Facebook and post your unique strengths. Share what you've learned about yourself and your unique strengths. Share how you intend to start using your strengths more often in the key areas of your life. Leave feedback of support on someone else's post.

—6—

CHOOSE YOUR REACTIONS

THE SYNAPSES THAT FIRE TOGETHER WIRE TOGETHER

"Never surrender your hopes and dreams to the fateful limitations others have placed on their own lives. The vision of your true destiny does not reside within the blinkered outlook of the naysayers and the doom prophets. Judge not by their words, but accept advice based on the evidence of actual results. Do not be surprised should you find a complete absence of anything mystical or miraculous in the manifested reality of those who are so eager to advise you. Friends and family who suffer the lack of abundance, joy, love, fulfillment, and prosperity in their own lives really have no business imposing their self-limiting beliefs on your reality experience."
—ANTHON ST. MAARTEN

There are many things in life that we cannot control. What we can control is our reaction to them. We can control what things mean to us. We can choose not to live with a victim mentality. When something goes wrong, we can't necessarily control the circumstances but we can always control how it affects us. We can choose happiness. We can choose to live in the Abundance State.

This doesn't mean we won't get down or get depressed, anxious, pessimistic, nervous, fearful, angry, and unhappy . . . it means that we won't stay there.

We will always have experiences and emotions that make us slip into a scarcity state. It doesn't matter how evolved and enlightened we are, we will battle our limiting beliefs and emotions every single day of our lives.

We must train our brains to bounce back to the Abundance State. We must *decide* to do this. Did you hear that? That's the key. The secret to cultivating the Abundance State is simply our decision to so. The practice of doing so rewires our brains so that, over time, it becomes easier and easier to do.

In the beginning, this will be hard because we're breaking years, maybe even decades of programming that's become cemented into our brains. But when we focus mindfully on doing this, on always recognizing when we're in a limiting state and choosing to snap back to an empowered state, it starts to become hardwired in our brains.

The best way to accomplish this is to gain clarity on our desired outcomes. When we're clear on the overarching, big-picture outcome we desire, we're less inclined to react with our emotional impulse. If we focus on directing all of our communications, including our self-dialogue, toward our big-picture desired outcomes, our relationships with others and with ourselves improve dramatically because we're not allowing limiting emotions to drive our behavior. When we control our electrochemical brain response to stimuli, we can rewire our brains to strengthen this impulse resistance.

All of the thoughts we have and the emotions we feel are the result of electrical signals firing over chemical bridges from one synapsis in our brains to another. These synapses form neural networks. In our lives, we tend to develop a pattern of thinking, and overtime this pattern is cemented in our neural networks. The physical structure of our brains actually changes to make it easier for us to feel the things that we have always felt and think the things we've always thought. This also makes it harder to feel and think in new ways.

In neuroscience, there's a theory called Hebbian theory, developed by Donald Hebb in his book *The Organization of Behavior*. I'll attempt to explain this as best I can.

All throughout our brains, we have synapses that are separated by empty space called a synaptic cleft, like a ravine. When we have a thought, one synapsis fires a chemical across this cleft, where it is received by another synapsis, forming a bridge that allows an electrical signal to pass over it. This electrical signal carries all the pertinent information in the thought that we experience. This is similar to the way nerves work when you stub your toe and the signal travels all the way to your brain where you actually feel it.

Neuroscientists use the phrase, "The synapses that fire together wire together." When two or more synapses become accustomed to sending signals to each other, they grow stronger and form neural networks, allowing the information they're sharing to pass more quickly and efficiently between them. The synaptic cleft literally closes in; decreasing the distance the signal needs to travel. The more times you respond to stimuli with limiting beliefs and limiting emotions, the more likely you are to continue to respond that way in the future. You are building a strong neural network responsible for negative and limiting patterns of thought.

To illustrate this effect, consider the following metaphor:

Imagine two pairs of people throwing a baseball to each other. One pair is standing ten feet apart, and the other is standing fifty feet apart. If they throw the ball at the same time, which one will arrive first? Clearly, the pair that is closer together.

This is an ultra-simplistic metaphor, but the point I'm making is that our brains have a mechanism to ensure that the themes we've created in our lives, through our repeated thoughts and emotions, arrive faster as well. If we are constantly angry or depressed or pessimistic, the synapses responsible for sending and receiving these signals grow stronger and closer. If we are cheerful, happy, and positive, these synapses will grow stronger and closer. Our brains physically change to accommodate our recurring thought patterns. This is how we learn and how memories are formed as well. It's called long-term potentiation (LTP).

If our thoughts can actually change the physical structure of our brains, then our thoughts can also change the external structures of our lives . . . our very reality. This is also known as the Constructionist Principle, and is one of the core factors that make up the foundation of Appreciative Inquiry.

When we constantly think in the same ways, it becomes harder and harder to react differently to events. When things happen in our lives, our brains are not only programmed to respond in a certain way, but the physical structure of our brains has been morphed in a way that games the system so it's harder to respond any other way.

Knowing this, if you had to choose between thinking with limiting beliefs and emotions or empowering beliefs and emotions, which would you choose?

The good news is we can make this choice at any time. We can rewire our brains very easily and it doesn't take that long.

It just requires us to focus on our desired emotions every day, to decide to live in a different state. To decide that, every time a limiting emotion or belief enters our mind, we'll immediately kick its ass out and choose to replace it with an empowering emotion or belief, regardless of what's going on around us.

> # CALL TO ACTION
>
> FOR A VIDEO ON HOW TO DO THIS, WATCH "CONVERTING LIMITS TO EMPOWERMENTS" IN THE PERSONAL EVOLUTION PLAN ONLINE.

Refuse to suffer. Take life in stride, knowing that with everything that happens, we either win or we learn and grow. There is no loss. Pain is inevitable in life, but suffering does not have to be. Not suffering is a choice that we can make when we choose happiness and fulfillment.

Decide every day that you are going to focus on the emotions that allow you to constantly live in an Abundance State. These emotions include love, acceptance, gratitude, curiosity, appreciation, bravery, contribution, cheerfulness, positivity, and determination. If you do this, you will build stronger connections in your brain. New synapses will begin to fire together, and like they say, "Synapses that fire together wire together." Do this and you will become an entirely better person, an evolved person.

When we actually operate from this state, we do not have to focus on every decision we make. Our decisions automatically flow from the state itself.

Let me give an example most people will understand. Have you ever gone on a diet? I'm guessing the answer is yes. Well, if you've been on a diet or tried to lose weight and are like most people, you've probably failed. A primary reason you've failed is because, rather than deciding you are going to operate from a state of determination, anchoring your mind in determination, and allowing determination to drive you, you attempt to stay the course from your default state. The problem is, your default state is ever changing and comprised of a substantial number of limiting beliefs and emotions.

In this limited state, every decision you have to make all day, every day, about what and when to eat and exercise becomes more and more difficult to manage. When your flag is on the line with every decision and you have no concrete emotional fortitude to shore up your will power, you are destined to fail. This is why the vast majority of people do fail when it comes to accomplishing their goals.

Conversely, if you make the conscious decision to operate using the empowering emotion of determination, every decision you make will be easier, because it is derived from your determined state of mind. When you are determined, your will power increases exponentially.

It's important to recognize that I'm not talking about simply telling yourself that you are determined. I'm talking about curating a state of mind rooted in the determination emotion. This is very different and requires a commitment to change. It sounds difficult but it's actually very easy, if you simply decide to do it. That's what it's all about. Your decision to be different.

Most people don't realize they can make this decision. Many don't even realize there's a decision to be made. They go through life believing that they are who they are, that their personality determines how they react, and that their emotional state is a constantly changing semi-uncontrollable condition of life. This is utterly false.

Your emotional state is not only fully controllable and able to be mastered, it's easy to do. Here's how . . . ready? Decide it's easy! Decide to do it! Done!

Say the following statement to yourself out loud:

"I am the master of my emotions. While I cannot control all of the events in my life or all of the things that happen to me, I can control how they affect me. I will control how they affect me. I choose to eliminate all limiting beliefs and emotions. I

choose to live in a loving, accepting, grateful, curious, appre-
ciative, brave, peaceful, cheerful, positive, and determined state
of mind. This is the Abundance State of Mind. This is not only
possible, it is a fact. It is a fact because I decide it is. I am un-
limited because I decide I am."

REPEAT, REPEAT, REPEAT! Eventually, this becomes en-grained in your subconscious and begins to manifest.

When you feel yourself slipping into anger, depression, uncer-tainty, fear, jealousy, resentment, or pessimism, slow down, close your eyes, take a deep breath, and repeat this statement. Then *de-cide* that your brain is reset and you are determined to live in the Abundance State.

Another method for maintaining a positive Abundance State is something called the five-minute rule. I learned this from my friend and mentor, Hal Elrod, bestselling author of *The Miracle Morning*. If you haven't read this book, I highly recommend it.

Essentially, in *The Miracle Morning*, Hal takes the daily ritu-als of the world's most successful people and performs them all in the morning, before the start of the day. These rituals he calls life SAVERS, which is an acronym for Silence (meditation), Affirma-tions, Visualization, Exercise, Reading, and Scribing (journaling). The concept is that the morning is the rudder of the day, and if you master your morning, you'll be more likely to master your day. Doing this was life changing for me, and for many others I know.

Anyway, the five-minute rule goes like this. When something happens to you that throws you into a negative emotional state, allow yourself five minutes to dwell in your pain. Five minutes to feel that anger, hurt, frustration, embarrassment; whatever it may be. Stew in it for five minutes. Live the feeling; let it take you over. Then, when five minutes is up, throw it away and replace it with an empowering emotion. Replace it with resolve, with determination, with love, with gratitude, with cheer. Replace it with purpose.

You may ask how in the world can you just replace a feeling? How can you just switch your feelings like a water faucet, changing from hot to cold? I have a very simple technique for doing this that we will discuss in the next chapter.

FROM UNFULFILLED TO UNLIMITED:

ELIMINATE FEAR AND CURATE ABUNDANCE THROUGH COURAGE AND CURIOSITY

"Man often becomes what he believes himself to be. If I keep on saying to myself that I cannot do a certain thing, it is possible that I may end by really becoming incapable of doing it. On the contrary, if I have the belief that I can do it, I shall surely acquire the capacity to do it even if I may not have it at the beginning."
—MAHATMA GANDHI

It may seem obvious but let me say it anyway. Happiness is not an action; it's an idea. If you look up happiness in the dictionary, it only exists in noun form. Meaning there is no verb or action for happiness. It's merely a concept. An emotion. An empowering emotion! It's the *result* of an action, not an action itself.

So how do you achieve happiness? By taking action, of course. By taking measured, intentional, and essential action that's in alignment with your values, unique strengths, and priorities, with a Radical Vision for the future and toward a meaningful purpose.

To most effectively accomplish this, you must have an understanding of your Positive Core, which again, is your values, strengths, and priorities. Then the basic pieces of *where* you're going and *why* you're going there are in place. The final piece is *how* you're going to get there. That's the taking action part, the hard part.

When I decided to write this book and launch a business with the mission of "being integral to the evolution of humanity," I sat down and analyzed the character traits that drive me—what I'm excellent at, and what I wanted out of life. In other words, my Positive Core. What came out of this analysis, as you know, is the Personal Evolution Plan. Once I knew where I wanted to go and why I wanted to go there, I began taking immediate action. Without action, you have a personal evolution *statement*, not a *plan*. Without action, your plans will go nowhere.

It may seem overwhelming to figure out what steps to take to manifest a truly radical future. It's not. You accomplish it by ensuring that you are always acting in alignment with your Positive Core and seeing your Radical Vision as a guiding star, not a distant shore.

Recognize that you only have to move in a direction, not to a destination. The destination reveals itself as you learn, grow, and reiterate. Staying true to your Positive Core in the actions you've been taking will magnetize you, and your vision will begin pulling you in. Rather than pushing against resistance, you're now being pulled, as if you were traveling downstream on a river.

Before this giant magnet can begin to exert its pull on you, you must begin developing into the person that attracts the level of success you desire. You do this by pushing against the massive resistance that holds most people back. You do this through the principles we've already discussed. Replacing your fear with bravery and curiosity, converting your limiting beliefs and emotions to empowering ones, and taking action by using Personal Evolution Plan to live with purpose.

What I've discovered on my own journey from unfulfilled to unlimited is that, no matter how committed I am to my decision to live in an Abundance State, there are always events in my life that are going to trigger limiting beliefs and emotions. This is due to the fact that fear is persistent and ingrained in us.

Fear is the root of every decision or indecision that chips away at our dreams and leaves us wanting for more. Its seed creeps into our psyche at a young age, and its roots invade every corner of our being. Left unchecked, fear will ruin us all.

Fear is the greatest limit of humanity. It always has been and it always will be.

Our brains were wired more for our survival, protection from predators, than they were for happiness. Early man relied on fear as a protection mechanism. The fight or flight response generated by fear was early man's best defense.

Fear in the modern world, however, is essentially useless to us. While we still benefit from the fight or flight response, it is clear that we as a species have reached a point where fear is a far greater hindrance to human potential than it is a cure for human weakness. It is one of those building blocks of humanity that we can't evolve out of fast enough.

We should not be kind in our treatment of fear. We should ostracize it, sending it as far to the edge of our consciousness as we can. When we feel it creeping in, we should run toward it with a warrior-like intensity. With our arms outstretched and our voices

CLOSER THAN YOU THINK

booming. Scare the shit out of fear and force it to retreat into the recesses of our being, where it belongs.

This is what every successful person I know does. Feel the fear but take action anyway. In fact, the most successful people I know use fear as a measuring stick when deciding which direction to take. If something scares you, it may be an indication that it's exactly what you should be doing. I challenge you to adopt this ethos. When something scares you, run into it. Doing this can be the single most life changing decision you ever make.

Courage is not a lack of fear; it's taking action in the face of it. The greatest cures for fear are courage and curiosity. Have the courage to be driven forward by your Radical Vision in the face of fear. And navigate the path through your fear by asking yourself the right questions, curiosity. Questions like, "What do I need to do to materialize my Radical Vision?" "How can facing this fear help me grow?" "How might I turn failure into an asset?"

Your fear of not realizing your vision should be greater than any other fear you have. Tie yourself to your vision. Define your future by your Radical Vision, and today's fear will pale in comparison to the fear of not realizing it.

Can you tell I hate fear? You should too! I can guarantee it's hurt you more than helped you by a wide margin. Did you know that there are only two natural fears? That is, fears that humans are born with. The rest are learned. The two natural fears are falling and loud noises. That's it! If you are afraid of anything other than these two things, then you have learned to be afraid of it. You can unlearn this as well.

Our submission to fear, and the limiting emotions and beliefs that result, have been built into the human condition throughout our evolution. We must place essential focus on overcoming them.

As we discussed earlier, our culture is created by and adapted through the conversations we have and the stories we tell. If you look at the stories we've told throughout history, humans have always viewed the world through the lens of scarcity. The picture of the future has always been bleak. Until quite recently, life expectancy was ridiculously short and disaster was always imminent. We did what we had to do so we could be prepared for the inevitable calamity that would soon be thrust upon us.

We did not see the world in terms of opportunity and abundance. The world was scary and unknowable, at least for the masses. Many of our ancient stories, especially those in our religious texts, depict a worldview that is representative of the expectations and fears of the people who wrote them. Those people had a fixed mindset saw the world through scarcity and fear. We've seen this permeate our political culture today, resulting in divisive actions based in fear.

Our stories are always a reflection of our inner world. This is why it's so important to cultivate one that's in alignment with how you want to see your outside world. Rather than trying to change *things*, change your *thoughts* and *beliefs*. Beliefs are the single most important factor in our lives. They decide our reality.

There's a great TED talk I watched, given by John Green, called "The nerd's guide to learning everything online." John talks about the idea of a "paper town" on a map. He explains, when cartographers make maps, often times they will create fake towns in order to protect their copyright. John states, because my map of New York and your map of New York will look very similar on account of the shape of New York, we will insert a fake place on our maps to prove that it is our work. This way, if my fake place shows up on your map, then I can be sure that you've ripped me off. Make sense?

Well in the case of this story, the cartographers at General Drafting created a fake town on their map called Agloe, New York. Agloe was just the two mapmakers' initials put together. The town did not actually exist.

Decades later, Rand McNally put out a map of New York, and guess what? Agloe, NY, appeared on the map. Well, the people at

General Drafting assumed they had been robbed, and contacted Rand McNally about it.

This is where it gets interesting. Rand McNally insisted that Agloe, NY, actually existed, that it is in fact a real town, and they were right!

Because this town existed on a map, people kept going there, expecting to see the town of Agloe. So someone actually built the town of Agloe. It had a gas station and a general store and everything.

This story makes a great metaphor. If our maps can actually create our terrain, then what can our beliefs create? After all, our beliefs are nothing more than the mental maps of our realities. We can choose to draw our maps in ways that manifest our desired reality outcomes, and, in the same way Agloe was built because it existed on a map of New York, we will construct what exists on the map of our reality. This is the power of belief.

Remember, it is our beliefs that hold all the power in our lives. We have to decide the things we want and believe we will have them. Any doubt only serves to keep them away or extend the time it takes for us to obtain them. All achievement begins with visualization. If you can't visualize the outcome, you will not achieve it.

I use curiosity to do this. I ask myself, "What is it that I *must* believe for me to manifest this Radical Vision?" Then I write down those beliefs. I then find *supporting facts* to hold up these empowering beliefs. I draw from times in my life where I was successful and when I achieved my goals.

Then I ask myself another question. "What are the *essential actions* that I must take on a daily basis to manifest my vision?" I write out the essential functions and actions that need to occur, and I immediately go to work on them.

That is the key—take immediate action. When you do this, your fears will begin to subside as you begin to see your empowering beliefs materialize in front of you.

It all starts with asking yourself the right questions. The quality of your life will never exceed the quality of your questions. This is the trick to converting your beliefs and emotions. You want to frame your questions in a way that's designed to illicit high-potential responses. The Six Fundamental Questions are the perfect example of this. Can you think of any other powerful questions you can ask yourself that will lead to growth and evolution?

In addition to using curiosity and asking yourself better questions, it's an important to curate an environment that inspires growth and determination. What I mean by this is removing the negative symbols, events, news, and people from your life as best you can.

I'm not suggesting you end friendships or alienate family. I'm saying that you need to marginalize the things in your life that don't directly inspire you to be better. If it doesn't bring you up, it brings you down. Eliminate neutral from your life. This is where mediocrity lives. Until you have the emotional intelligence to deal with these things properly, marginalize them.

One of the things I did that had a huge impact was changing my Facebook newsfeed. I know it may sound ridiculous, but it really worked. I noticed my newsfeed was full of people complaining, political arguments, hateful or negative memes, etc. I got to work on actively changing this.

I found the public figures who inspired me and liked their pages. I friend requested people on the periphery of my circle of positive friends and connections. I joined a couple of groups dedicated to gratitude where everyday people posted what they were grateful for, and I started making similar posts. Before I knew it, my feed was full of inspiring, determined, positive people doing inspiring, determined, and positive things.

I didn't have to avoid Facebook to avoid negativity anymore. I could engage even more on Facebook and get more out of it. Build new connections, learn, and love more.

I also dedicated myself to the practice of meditation. There are a million ways to meditate, and I'm not going to endorse one over another. First, I'm not qualified to and, second, I believe any form of meditation to be far superior to the alternative of not meditating. Personally, I practice Transcendental Meditation (TM), which is a mantra-based mediation. Many people believe they can't meditate because they can't clear their minds of thoughts. This is missing the point. You're not supposed to clear your mind of thoughts. This goes against the very nature of the mind. That's what attracted to me to TM. You focus on a mantra but understand that your mind will wander into thoughts. This is where your nervous system is releasing stress and relaxing. When you become aware that you've lost the mantra and are having thoughts, you easily return to the mantra. This happens dozens or hundreds of times during the mediation, and it's not only okay, it's the entire point of it.

The simple act of mindfulness, taking the time to be present in the moment and just exist, just be, is life changing. Meditation and mindfulness can change your entire state of mind permanently.

For many, it builds up that space between stimulus and response. That space where something happens, and you may not always be able to control your first impulse. But you're mindful enough to not react and allow your second thought, your mindful thought, to be the one you put out there.

The importance of this cannot be overstated. So many of us have responded, throughout our lives, in ways that we are not proud of. So many of us just react to what's happening without taking the time to be aware of what we want our reaction to be. Or maybe we didn't know how to react to a situation, only to realize later what we should have done, when it was too late. Many people continue to do this and think that it's just the way of life, that there's no alternative to reacting to the moment. Are you one of these people?

Meditation expands the space between stimulus and reaction. It builds your emotional intelligence to a point where you can ignore your negative impulse and decide your appropriate response. Practicing this over and over again works to rewire your brain so that, with time, your impulse actually changes.

When you no longer require the space created by meditation for impulse control, you can use it to master your world. To evolve.

—8—

FUNDAMENTAL QUESTION # 3

WHAT ARE MY PRIORITIES AND MOTIVATIONS?

"Most of us spend too much time on what is urgent and not enough time on what is important."
—STEPHEN R. COVEY

D o you have clear priorities outlined? If I ask you right now what your top five priorities are, would you be able to concisely articulate them? Chances are, you may struggle with this at first. Even though we all think we know what we want in life, it can be a challenging task to clearly define the order of importance of our desires.

After all, that's what priorities are. Things that are important for us to do or have. A thing, or things, that is regarded as more important than others. This is where having clarity on your desired outcomes and the ability to differentiate between the 80 percent of inconsequential noise in life from the 20 percent that drives results is paramount to your success.

CALL TO ACTION

GO TO WWW.PERSONALEVOLUTIONPLAN.COM AND COMPLETE
MODULE 3: PRIORITIES

WELCOME BACK FROM THE WEB!

In Module 3 of your Personal Evolution Plan, you answered more questions that were designed to trigger your brain to consider what is truly important to you.

Here's a recap of the questions we asked:

1. What is important for me to have in life?
2. Why is this important?
3. What is important for me to do in life?
4. Why is this important?
5. Who is important for me to have in my life?
6. What is important for me to do for them?
7. How will they be affected by what I want to do?
8. What images of the future cause me to most quickly and naturally come alive?

9. What emotions will I feel when I achieve my priorities?

10. How will my day-to-day life be different when I achieve this?

11. Are there opportunities to feel these emotions today, using what I already have, that can allow me to leverage more satisaction?

The real trick with priorities is to make sure they are in alignment with your Core Values and unique strengths. When you define your priorities in alignment with these, it is much more likely that your priorities will be realized in your life. For example, if I value curiosity and one of my strengths is communication, then I may choose to set a priority of learning new things and teaching them to others. In this way, I have a much greater likelihood of accomplishing my priority.

If your priorities are random and not tied to your values, then you will lack the emotional context to manifest your priorities in your life.

It is also important not to confuse priorities with goals. Priorities are broad concepts. Just as values are broad ideas that inform our decisions, priorities are broad desires that inform our direction. In other words, priorities are what's important for us in life overall not just in the moment.

Before the Personal Evolution Plan became the well-devised system that it is today, I was sitting with my journal and trying to figure out how I was going to change my life. I started with my priorities. I jotted down the things that I wanted in life. Things like to raise happy and healthy kids, to do work that fulfills me, to care for the needs of my family, to earn a lot of money, etc.

These are all great priorities, and most of them are still on my list. But what I should have done, and what I ended up doing, is start with my values. My values are my why. Why I do what I do.

I realized, after a couple weeks of journaling and thinking about everything I had written, that the values are the clear starting point.

It is not until we have a clear understanding of our why (values), that we can consider our what (priorities), with the emotional context required to manifest them in our lives.

I'm talking about values again now because it is both fundamental and paramount that, when creating your priorities, you are carefully considering how they align with your values. If you cannot justify what you want with why you want it, then you will never be satisfied.

This is because the things we want aren't actually things. They're feelings. We don't want the thing itself; we want the feeling it gives us. If we establish a priority then set and accomplish a goal which manifests that priority in our lives, but the priority wasn't rooted in our why, we will feel empty inside. We won't be fulfilled because what we've achieved will not give us the feelings we desire. Not for any lasting period of time, anyway. Remember, this happened to me and triggered my very own hero's journey.

But when our priorities are firmly rooted in our why, when we accomplish goals that make our priorities a reality, we feel a deep sense of fulfillment. As Tony Robbins says, "Success without fulfillment is the ultimate failure."

YOUR POSITIVE CORE

Now that you've completed the first three of the Six Fundamental Questions, you should have a deep, contextual understanding of your Positive Core (values, strengths, and priorities).

This is the essence of you. It is what brings life to you and to those you impact. It's how you make meaning in and of the world. It is the root cause of your success. As long as you commit to being the embodiment of your Positive Core in everything that you do, with everyone you come into contact with, you will be able to amplify the good, annihilate the bad, and create any future that you can dream and imagine.

In the next chapter, we're going to answer the Fourth Fundamental Question—**What might a Radical Vision of a truly fulfilling life look life?** Now may be a good time to go back through the Personal Evolution Plan online and read through your notes. Make sure you have a firm grasp on the values, unique strengths, and priorities that make up your Positive Core. This is what you'll use to dream up a radical, fulfilling future.

9

FUNDAMENTAL QUESTION #4

WHAT MIGHT A RADICAL VISION OF A TRULY FULFILLING LIFE LOOK LIKE?

"Your beliefs become your thoughts,
Your thoughts become your words,
Your words become your actions,
Your actions become your habits,
Your habits become your values,
Your values become your destiny."
—MAHATMA GANDHI

WHAT IS A LIFE OF PURPOSE? WHAT DOES THAT REALLY MEAN?

There's a lot of talk about purpose these days. It's become a buzzword. Particularly in the business world, where we're seeing a renaissance of companies defining themselves through the purpose they serve and enjoying the highest level of success in their respective industries.

Purpose, by definition, means "the reason for which something exists." This can get pretty deep. We're going to take a different approach when it comes to how we discuss purpose and define it for ourselves, which is what we really need to consider when we're designing a Radical Vision for the future.

Rather than getting lost in a philosophical rabbit hole in an attempt to discover the very nature of our existence, we're going to be more practical in the way we view and understand purpose. We're going to take a utilitarian view of it, if you will.

As I said in Chapter 1, I believe the reason the vast majority of people are unhappy, unfulfilled, and disengaged at their core is because they refuse to allow themselves to dream. They don't feel it's appropriate to have a Radical Vision of the future. They were compelled by the communities and institutions they grew up in to conform, to be like each other rather than to be radical.

The key to cultivating happiness, fulfillment, and abundance in life is to craft a Radical Vision of your future based on your dreams of an ideal life. Remember when people are asked what they would do if money were no object, most say they would focus on growth and contribution. This is evidence that many of us know somewhere inside of us how to be happy, we just struggle navigating the path of doing so. This is why I developed the Personal Evolution Plan.

Let me share a little about my path, my personal evolution. In my radical future, I spend my days creating shared prosperity in the world by teaching people to envision and become the best versions of themselves through essential action in alignment with their values, unique strengths, and priorities—otherwise known as the Positive Core—to create marketable solutions that fulfill global needs.

In my version of an abundant future, we no longer sit back and wait for the government or corporations to solve the world's problems. But rather, we work together through social networks, both virtual and physical, using crowdsourcing to gather the necessary people and capital required to effect massive change in our own lives, in our communities, and around the world. Our personal evolutions form a collective strength that acts as dominoes that can knock down even the most oppressive obstacles.

This Radical Vision of a truly fulfilling life for me not only satisfies my foundational and elevating needs (*certainty, hope, connection,* and *significance, growth* and *contribution*) but it is generated directly from the deployment of my Positive Core in the world. All of my values, all of my unique strengths and talents, and all of my priorities are actively engaged in ways that allow the best of me to emerge. This is the key to dreaming and imagining a Radical Vision of a truly fulfilling life.

What is it about the life that *you* envision that brings you the joy, happiness, and fulfillment that you truly desire? Imagine that life. What would you be doing for work? For fun? For growth and contribution? Where would you be living? How much money would you have? How much do you really need? What emotions do you want to feel the most?

The answers to these questions are going to inform you when designing your Radical Vision. To better understand what a Radical Vision is, consider the words independently. Radical means a change to the fundamental nature of something. Vision is a mental image of what the future will look like.

Your radical vision means to fundamentally change your mental image of your future. To see yourself living an abundant life, using all of your values, your unique strengths, and your priorities in ways that add ultimate value to yourself and to the world. This must be crafted without today's limits. You must empower yourself while crafting your Radical Vision to remove all of your current limits and imagine what an abundant future could look like in a perfect world without the possibility of failure or limitation.

Do not be afraid of deciding on a grand radical vision. Remember Peter Diamandis? Don't allow the limiting belief that you don't deserve to live such a grand idea, or that you aren't capable of living such a rich life, prevent you from designing the boldest, most Radical Vision you can. Use the techniques we covered earlier to convert these limiting beliefs to empowering ones, and be courageous!

The truth is, most people when faced with the actuality of living a bold life of deep purpose become paralyzed by fear and insecurity. They fear that they are not good enough. They fear that they don't deserve it. They fear that they may be exposed as an imposter. They fear that they will fail publicly and be humiliated.

All of us, myself included, even the most successful people, I know feel this fear. The difference between people who succeed and live lives of unlimited happiness and fulfillment and those who don't is that we don't let it stop us.

Don't let it stop you. Decide now to leave life as a member of the unhappy, unfulfilled, and disengaged majority behind and join the few unlimited people living with mastery.

Reprogram your brain and your body to push through the fear and act anyway. This is where you grow. It is at the end of the comfort zone where life begins. If you never leave your comfort zone, you are as good as dead.

After a while, you will start to chase this fear. You'll be a fear slayer. Because you'll know that when you feel fear, and you run toward it with intensity, you are becoming a person who is capable of anything. You are becoming who you want to be. The things you do when you're afraid will determine the person you become.

It may take some time for your Radical Vision to take shape. That's okay. You're not supposed to be able to see everything all at once.

Start by calling up images that cause you to most come alive, to feel the highest sense of pride, joy, and fulfillment. Know that with time and action, your vision will become clearer as it morphs and takes shape. Here are some provocative questions to get you started:

1. What part of my life or work do I enjoy the most today?

2. In what ways can I reinvent myself to better utilize my highest strengths?

3. What purpose and motivations drive me more than any other? In what ways can I imagine this evolving?

4. How can I strengthen my connection to my Positive Core?

5. What visions of the future cause me to most quickly and naturally come alive?

6. What aspects of this vision give me the greatest sense of joy, energy, and pride?

7. What pain or void exists or has existed in me that I can help others repair, fill, or avoid?

8. If I could go into the future, one, three, or five years from now, what would excellence look like?

SAMPLE RADICAL VISION STATEMENT:

The best version of myself (does) _____ so that _____, thus _____.

Example (from Mike): *The best version of myself <u>teaches people, organizations, and communities Positive Core Mapping and Radical Visioning</u> so that <u>they can create collective wisdom, and shared prosperity, by adding their highest value to world,</u> thus <u>hastening the evolution of humanity.</u>*

Go ahead and write down your own Radical Vision statement. You can use the framework in the example above, or create your own. The more detailed the better. Just remember, this is what's important to you today. This may change. In fact it should. It should grow and evolve with you as you grow and evolve.

A major misconception I see around *purpose* is that many people think it's static. Like it's something to be found. Purpose isn't out there hiding and waiting for you to find it. It's dynamic. It's nothing more than the embodiment of your Positive Core today. It can, will, and should change over time.

CALL TO ACTION

Go to **WWW.PERSONALEVOLUTIONPLAN.COM** and complete
MODULE 4: Radical Vision

10

FUNDAMENTAL QUESTION #5

WHY WOULD MY RADICAL VISION LOOK LIKE THAT?

Once you've got the makings of your Radical Vision for the future, it's critical to draw out the themes that make it so. By taking the time to understand the characteristics inherent to your vision that most drive you, you'll be able to immediately put them to work in your life.

What is it about your radical, fulfilling future makes it so compelling? As with everything we've done thus far, asking yourself some provocative questions is the best way to extract the themes from your vision.

CALL TO ACTION

Go to WWW.PERSONALEVOLUTIONPLAN.COM and complete MODULE 5: Extracting Themes

Some questions you should consider are:

1. What is different in my future than it is today?
2. Who will I be adding value to in the future?
3. What will I get out of this?
4. How specifically will I embody my values in the future?
5. How do I bring all of my strengths to everything I do in the future?
6. How will I know when my priorities are met? When I am deeply fulfilled?
7. How will I satisfy my foundational human needs of *certainty, hope, connection,* and *significance*?
8. How will I self-actualize by satisfying my elevating needs of *growth* and *contribution*?
9. How will I measure the impact I'm making?
10. What qualities will drive me to make decisions?
11. Why is this future so important to me?

The answers to these questions will shine a light on what characteristics of a compelling future are most important to you.

Look over your answers and write down three to five themes that best describe your vision. These themes are the *guiding star* that you will take action toward, by maximizing your Positive Core every day, in everything that you do. If you build these themes into your daily life, your world will change immediately.

What I mean by this is, when you take actions that advance you down a new road in life by intentionally creating meaning, you start to build a new world around you. You create new pathways, or clear the brush so you can see those that have always existed. Over time, your surroundings are completely different. Your access to the things and the people you need to manifest your vision into your reality grows, and you begin to be pulled in your desired direction, rather than having to push your way there alone.

Your Radical Vision will change as you make progress toward it. It will grow in scope and impact and will develop extreme clarity through your mindfulness, essential focus, and action taking.

As we travel further down the path from unfulfilled to unlimited, through essential focus on growth and contribution our individual characteristics will change. They will adapt and assimilate to new information, new requirements, new demands, new ideas, new inspirations, and new callings.

Be open to this change. Run fast with your purpose but hold it loosely. Remain open to new and better versions of yourself, and always reassess how you are satisfying your foundational and elevating needs through your values, unique strengths, and priorities. Be mindful of how your purpose manifests itself in all the key areas of your life.

In order to clearly define your Radical Vision, you must first know what emotions you are seeking. You see, it's not the things we achieve that make us happy; it's the feelings our accomplishments give us. Decide what emotions you enjoy feeling, and design your life so you can feel them as often as possible. When you do this, you'll cultivate unlimited motivation, determination, and persistence.

One of my favorite of the quotes that hang on my office wall is by Calvin Coolidge. He says,

"Nothing in this world can take the place of persistence. Talent will not; nothing is more common than unsuccessful men with talent. Genius will not; unrewarded genius is almost a proverb. Education will not; the world is full of educated derelicts. Persistence and determination alone are omnipotent. The slogan Press On! has solved and always will solve the problems of the human race."

CALL TO ACTION

GO TO THE PERSONAL EVOLUTION TRIBE ON FACEBOOK AND POST YOUR RADICAL VISION STATEMENT. SHARE WHAT YOU'VE LEARNED ABOUT YOURSELF USING THE EXERCISES IN STEP 4. LEAVE FEEDBACK OF SUPPORT ON SOMEONE ELSE'S POST.

11

FUNDAMENTAL QUESTION #6

HOW MIGHT I GO ABOUT DESIGNING MY RADICAL, FULFILLING LIFE?

"If you have built castles in the air, your work need not be lost; that is where they should be. Now put the foundations under them."
—HENRY DAVID THOREAU

You've come a long way. So far, you've identified and drilled deep into your Core Values, your unique strengths, and your priorities. You've used these key characteristics to craft a Radical Vision for your future. You've taken the time to understand why that vision is so compelling to you. What you choose to do right now will impact the rest of your life.

Life usually comes down to a handful of major decisions and this is one of them. Right now, you need to make the decision to live your Radical Vision. You need to make the decision to live with purpose, to live without limits.

Many people will stop at this point in the book and course and never have the courage to set moonshot goals and take the actions necessary every day to accomplish them. I'm hoping you do have the courage to do this, because if you do, your life will never be the same. You will accomplish more than you ever thought possible. You will grow beyond your wildest dreams and have an impact on this world that will not be forgotten. This power is within you right now. At this point in the book, and in your Personal Evolution Plan online, you've been asked and (hopefully) answered a lot of questions. Now you're at the part of your very own hero's journey where you have to put it all together in ways that manifest change in your life and lead you to your desired outcomes.

Here's the good news: you've already done the hard work. The rest can be as easy or difficult as you make it. Let me explain. The question we're attempting to answer in this chapter may appear, to the vast majority of people, to be a daunting one. One that if it were so easy to answer, then all of their problems and the problems of the world would could be rendered irrelevant. Maybe so, or maybe not.

I've discovered a secret—perhaps you've picked up some of the breadcrumbs left throughout this book—and learned from the ways in which we've gotten to this final point. Here's the secret: *the answers to our most difficult questions are not as elusive as we think, but rather are hidden in the ways in which we frame the questions we ask.*

Our questions are fateful. Once an inquiry is made, the future is immediately and forever changed. This is because the questions we ask are the lenses through which we view our worlds. Just as when you put on a pair of glasses, you no longer look *at* the lens but *through* it. The lens becomes unperceivable, but your view of the world comes into focus. This is what a question does for your subconscious.

There's no such thing as a question without a consequence. There are no neutral questions. Every inquiry takes us on a journey. Poorly framed questions lead us back to where we began. How well we frame our inquiry determines where and how far we can go.

CALL TO ACTION

Go to WWW.PERSONALEVOLUTIONPLAN.COM and complete
MODULE 6: Igniting My Personal Evolution

Let's recap the questions we've asked so far on this journey:

1. Who am I?
2. What do I do?
3. Who do I do it for?
4. What do they need?
5. What do I get out of it?
6. Why is this important and what does this all mean?
7. What are some challenges I've faced in my life and how did I overcome them?
8. What do I like about myself?

9. What do people compliment me on?

10. What do I enjoy doing?

11. What am I proud of?

12. What is important for me to have in life?

13. Why is this important?

14. What is important for me to do in life?

15. Why is this important?

16. Who is important in my life?

17. What is it important for me to do for them?

18. How will they be affected by what I want to do?

19. How will my day-to-day life be different when I achieve this?

20. What emotions will I feel when I achieve my priorities?

21. Are there opportunities to feel these emotions today, using what I already have, that can allow me to leverage more satisfaction?

22. What part of my life or work today do I enjoy the most?

23. What purpose and motivations drive me more than any other?

24. In what ways can I imagine this evolving?

25. How can I strengthen my connection to my Positive Core?

26. What visions of the future cause me to most quickly and naturally come alive?

27. What aspects of this vision give me the greatest sense of joy, energy, and pride?

28. What pain or void exists or has existed in me that I can help others repair, fill, or avoid?

29. If I could go into the future, one, three, or five years from now, what would excellence look like?

30. What is different in my future than it is today?

31. Who will I be adding value to in the future?

32. What will I get out of this?

33. How, specifically, do I embody my values in the future?

34. How do I bring all of my strengths to everything I do in the future?

35. How will I know when my priorities are met? When I am deeply fulfilled?

36. How will I satisfy my foundational human needs of *certainty, hope, connection,* and *significance?*

37. How will I self-actualize by satisfying my elevating needs of *growth* and *contribution?*

38. How will I measure the impact I'm making?

39. What qualities will drive me to make decisions?

40. Why is this future so important to me?

The answers to questions 1-6, along with the exercises in Personal Evolution Plan Module 1, should have led you to identify your Core Values. You should have also asked the 5 Why's of your values to add weight to them. Write down what your Core Values are and why:

_____

_____

_____

_____

_____
_____

BONUS VALUES QUESTION:

In what situations do your Core Values come through, and in what situations can you do a better job of bringing them out?

_____
_____
_____
_____
_____
_____
_____

The answers to questions 7-11, along with the exercises in Personal Evolution Plan Module 2, should have led you to identify your *unique strengths*. Write down your unique strengths:

_____
_____
_____
_____
_____
_____
_____

BONUS STRENGTHS QUESTIONS:

In which areas of life do you best utilize your strengths, and in which areas do you allow them to take a backseat either to your own fear or to another person's strengths?

_____

_____

_____

_____

_____

_____

_____

_____

_____

What strengths are emerging in you? Which of those can you work to build and utilize to reinvent yourself?

_____

_____

_____

_____

_____

_____

_____

_____

_____

The answers to questions 12-22, along with the exercises in Personal Evolution Plan Module 3, should have led you to identify your *priorities* and *motivations*. Write down your priorities and motivations:

_____

_____

_____

_____

_____

_____

_____

_____

The answers to questions 23-40, along with the exercises in Personal Evolution Plan Modules 4 and 5, should have helped you identify your Radical Vision of a truly fulfilling life why it would look like that. Write down any insights and themes that you've been able to extract:

_____

_____

_____

_____

_____

_____

_____

You should have used your Positive Core and the insights gained from dreaming and imaging a truly fulfilling future to outline a Radical Vision Statement. Write your Radical Vision Statement here:

_____

_____

_____

_____

_____

_____

_____

_____

_____

All that is left to do at this point is to take measured, essential, and intentional action every day, deploying the best of your Positive Core in the direction of your guiding star (your Radical Vision). Easy, right? Let's address the elephant in the room.

Motivation comes easily. Change does too. You can change in an instant. It's maintaining the motivation and sustaining the change that's hard. I struggle with this all the time. It's the oldest problem in personal growth. Luckily, I've found a solution, and it's in Chapter 12.

—12—

MAINTAINING THE CHANGE

THE AVID PRACTICE

In the past, every time I went to a seminar or a mastermind meeting, saw a great speaker, read a fascinating book, or had a strong connection with someone inspiring, I'd walk away feeling empowered and motivated to go seize the day. But, inevitably, not having a concrete daily practice or ritual allowed that passion to fade away and the status quo to resume in my life. This is the case for most of us.

It's so easy to get motivated, to discover *what* to do. But what's less prevalent in personal development books and programs is the *why* and, most importantly, the *how.* What's most difficult is sustaining the momentum. I've solved this common problem by creating the practice of AVID.

AVID is your secret weapon that keeps you moving forward while others fail. It is the daily practice that I've created to combat the age-old problem of waning motivation. It's a grounding routine that ensures you are moving in the direction you wish to go.

WHAT IS AVID?

I've taken my own research and experience, combined with that of some of the top thought leaders, psychologists, neuroscientists, and straight-up life hackers I know of, to find a way to carry on the momentum of the motivation we feel when we become inspired, and not allow it to slip away. What resulted was easier and more efficient than I ever thought it could be. Welcome to AVID.

The Merriam-Webster Dictionary defines the word avid as:
"Characterized by enthusiasm and vigorous pursuit."

With great serendipity, this word that so perfectly describes how we should attack the status quo and seize a life of greatness, also forms the ideal acronym for the daily practice of doing just so.

AVID stands for:

- Anchor
- Visualize
- Intentional Action
- Debrief

The following instruction on the process of anchoring and visualizing may seem a bit overwhelming at first read. There's a lot of technical stuff here. Don't be discouraged. There's a course built into the Personal Evolution Plan that walks you through exactly how to do all of this. I challenge you, however, to go through the exercises below first, taking care with the details. Take your time. Repeat this as many times as you have to. This is one of the most powerful tools you'll ever learn.

ANCHOR

Anchoring is the process of switching yourself into a desired state of being. You can learn to do this in a very short amount of time.

Here's a quick exercise that will teach you the anchoring process.

Imagine a time when you were at your best. When you felt the happiest, proudest, most fulfilled, most excited, most alive.

Pull the images or movie of this event into your mind. See the colors, the shapes, and the environment around you in the image. Feel exactly what you felt in that moment, smell what you smelled, hear what you heard. Do so as vividly as possible. Anchoring is most powerful when you are recalling the event with all of your senses. Bring the image as close as you can, so that you can make out the finest details. Put yourself right back in that moment as it unfolds in your mind.

Now, at the height of the intensity of recalling this event with all your senses, set a trigger or stimulus. A trigger can be visual, kinesthetic, or auditory. In other words, you can press on the point between your thumb and pointer finger as a trigger. Maybe you are more auditory so you make a sound. If you're more visual, you may imagine a lever next to you that you grab and push all the way up, with the intensity of the event cresting at the highest position of the lever. The most effective triggers are ones that are comprised of all three modes.

Now that you've set a trigger at the height of the intensity of your memory, release it and change back to a neutral state. The best way to do this is to ask yourself a non-sequitur, like, "what am

I going to have for breakfast tomorrow?" Something to break the emotional state that you were just in and come back to the present. This change of state is extremely important for setting a clean stimulus/response anchor.

Now you can test your trigger to see if it worked. Repeat the trigger and see if it evokes the desired state (the positive emotions you felt when you set the trigger). Repeat this process until it does. This is called stacking the anchor. It may take three to five times for the trigger to evoke your desired state.

Once you have this down, it will literally change your life. This process can be used for anything from envisioning a future version of yourself and stepping into the traits of that person, to overcoming a past hardship, to breaking bad habits and setting new ones.

There's a simple acronym for the process of anchoring known as RACE.

- Recall, recalling an event where you were at your best—the desired state.
- Anchor, setting the trigger at the height of intensity while reliving this event.
- Change, releasing the trigger and returning to a neutral state.
- Evoke, repeat the trigger to see if it causes the desired state.

SOME KEYS TO SETTING TRIGGERS

When setting triggers keep in mind ITURN.,

I - **Intensity:** Anchors work better when the desired state is also intense. Also, when it's a natural state, meaning it occurs naturally in your life. This is so you can set anchors in real time when the desired state occurs. This is a more advanced way to practice anchoring.

T - Timing: Set the trigger just before the peak intensity of the desired state is reached. Hold it until just before the state begins to diminish.

U - Uniqueness: Your trigger must be unique in the sense that it can't be something you do on a regular basis, such as shaking hands or nodding your head. It must be special in the sense that it is only tied to the desired state and not a part of your everyday activity.

R - Replication: You must be able to repeat the trigger with precision every time you try.

N - Number of times: This is also known as *stacking*. The more times you set the anchor, the more effective it will be.

VISUALIZE

The visualization component of AVID works by stacking the anchors you set to go to work for you in the future. When you established an anchor, you did so by recalling an event from your past where you were at your best. Now you're going to use that desired state you've evoked to visualize your future. See yourself living the most compelling images of your radical future. See yourself there, being the best version of yourself that you can imagine. See it, feel it, smell it, hear it.

See that future version of yourself standing in a square of color. Choose any color you wish. Whatever color symbolizes power and success for you. See that future-self standing in this colored square in front of you, and now step into the square. Step into your future body. You are now this person. Now visualize yourself going through your day as this person.

Now anchor this. Set a new trigger, different from your other trigger. Now you have a trigger to call up both the best of the past and the best of what's possible.

This process of anchoring and visualizing can be extremely powerful if you practice it regularly. Don't be overwhelmed by how complicated this seems. It's really easy when you practice it a few times. I promise.

INTENTIONAL ACTION

This is all about going through your day and remembering to take action that is both in alignment with your Positive Core, and also leading you toward your Radical Vision. It may help to ask yourself some powerful questions to determine which intentional actions are most appropriate for you.

These questions can include:

1. What is most important in life?
2. What is most important today? (Important distinction: this may be very different from your answer to question 1)
3. How would the best version of me show up today?
4. What are three to five things I can do to move closer to my Radical Vision today?
5. How can I best leverage my top strengths today?

Once you understand the key essential actions and functions that drive you toward your vision, you can check in with yourself throughout the day to see if you've moved closer to or further away from where you wish to go. Have you been intentional, focused on the 20 percent of actions that drive 80 percent of results, or have you allowed yourself to become sidetracked?

DEBRIEF

Debriefing is of ultimate importance. This is where you really learn, grow, and give yourself the opportunity to reiterate. At the end of the day, grab your journal and spend a few minutes asking yourself some provocative questions.

1. What are some images of today that I'm most proud of, excited by, and cause me to most come alive?

2. How have I moved closer to my Radical Vision today?

3. What values, strengths, and priorities are emerging in me today? In other words, what's showing up that's new or unexpected that I may have an opportunity to build upon?

4. How did I apply my Positive Core successfully today?

5. What is most important for tomorrow?

You can add to, subtract from, or alter any of these questions in any way that works for you. Super powerful stuff comes from this daily practice.

A FINAL NOTE

I want to leave you with a personal story from my mortgage banker days. I was on a call with my business coach, and I had been telling him for the past couple of months that I wanted to branch out of production and start recruiting to build my own branch of the company.

For a couple weeks in a row, he asked me what I had done for recruiting that week, and I always had an excuse as to why I hadn't gotten started yet. On this particular call, I reiterated that recruiting was a priority to me, and he cut me off by saying, "No it's not."

I wasn't sure how to respond, so I asked him what made him think that. His response was so simple and true, but I hadn't considered it before. He said, "If it was a priority, you would be doing it. The fact that you aren't doing it means it's not a priority, Mike. It's that simple. Have you looked up the definition of priority?"

All I could say in response was, "You're right. I guess it's not a priority right now." Then it became very clear to me. If I wasn't taking action on this, then maybe it really wasn't that important to me. Maybe I was just trying to find new avenues to pursue without taking the time to carefully consider whether or not they were things I was really prepared to do at that time.

I was taking up valuable brainpower thinking about recruiting when it really wasn't essential for me at that particular time. It reminds me of a favorite Bruce Lee quote, "It is not a daily increase, but a daily decrease. Hack away at the inessentials."

I share this with you because I want you to make sure the goals you set are things that you really want. Something that's going to get you up early and keep you up late. Something that's going to drive you, and fill you with joy. Most importantly, make sure you are actually prepared to do the things necessary to accomplish your goals. Be honest with yourself, and don't take on things you aren't prepared for. Set goals that you know you will accomplish because your passion gives you no other choice.

Setting and accomplishing goals is what sets apart the truly successful and happy people from everyone else. I've never met a successful person who didn't set and accomplish goals religiously.

Accomplishing goals is addictive. When you get that first win, you want to repeat that feeling over and over again. You'll build off of each win with bigger and more audacious goals. Before you know it, you'll be mastering your world, changing lives, and living in the Abundance State. So start small, and start now!

WRAP UP AND NEXT STEPS

I hope you found this book useful. The content is a compilation of all the best advice, tools, techniques, and insights that have inspired me from the various coaches, mentors, speakers, strategists, and personal-development professionals I've either worked with directly or looked up to in my life. I have combined that with modern neuroscience and psychology research, Appreciative Inquiry, my own personal experience, and the actual process that I created for myself to obtain a major paradigm shift in my own life.

I believe, if you took this book to heart and put your best effort into it, that you are well on your way to a radical Personal Evolution.

I'm hoping you'll take advantage of The Personal Evolution Tribe, as this is a free resource. Nothing is sold in this group, but rather, like-minded travelers on the path from unfulfilled to unlimited share extreme value. This is a place where you can grow your network to build a platform, and you can add your own value to the world.

Just go to https://www.facebook.com/groups/personalevolutiontribe and request to join the Tribe if you're not already a member.

I want to point out that the Personal Evolution Plan is designed in the order it is for a reason. When we start with our values first and really drill down on them using the 5-Why's exercise, everything else becomes clearer. As we progress through the process, having this deep understanding of our values makes it easy to define our priorities with the clarity of mind necessary to ensure our Radical Vision is rooted in sustainable ground. And that it speaks to what drives us so personally, that it's impervious to the brutal onslaught it will take from the outside world as we erect the pillars of abundant greatness in our lives.

If you actually do the things you promised yourself you would while reading this book and taking the course, your life is about to become very difficult. This difficulty is temporary, but you need to expect that it's coming so you have the tools to deal with it. If you can persist through it, your life will be greatly improved.

There is inertia in us all that we must fight relentlessly. It's a force that prevents us from seeing ourselves as great, as deserving, as extremely capable individuals who have the power to manifest any emotion and outcome we choose. Overcoming this inertia takes persistence and determination. It also takes a community. You absolutely must surround yourself with people on the same path as you and use them for support while you give them the same.

I also strongly urge you to get a coach or a mentor. Whether that's me or anyone else who can help, please find one. You don't have to spend a lot of money on this. I have a group coaching and mastermind program designed around the principles in this book that nearly anyone can afford.

I'm not saying this as a marketing ploy to get you to buy into my coaching program, I'm saying it because I know from personal experience how much support you're going to need to sustain a radical change in your life. Making change is easy. Sustaining it is the hard part. There are a ton of great mentors and coaches out there. Make sure you're working with one.

The first two months of action are the hardest. If you can get through the early days of confusion and doubt with your determination and intensity intact, then your odds of succeeding are exponentially improved. Just focus on your AVID practice, and it will carry you through. I highly urge you to take the 30-Day Radical Vision Challenge.

CLOSER THAN YOU THINK

THE 30-DAY RADICAL VISION CHALLENGE

Can you completely reinvent yourself and see real-world results in thirty days? The answer is absolutely yes.

Cultivating the mindset and taking the measured, essential, and intentional action to manifest your vision into reality only requires you to answer yes to the following questions. So, let's take a crack at it. Ready?

1. Do you want to be better tomorrow than you are today?

If yes, proceed to the next question.

2. Are you committed to taking full responsibility for doing this?

If yes, see below.

If you're still reading that means you answered yes to wanting to be better tomorrow than you are today, and that you are committed to taking full responsibility for doing the things necessary to accomplish this.

The 30-Day Radical Vision Challenge is designed to help you build the neural pathways you need to maintain the motivation and sustain the change to manifest your Radical Vision.

This is done by the use of a daily routine. Remember, the synapses that fire together, wire together. Thirty days is the perfect amount of time to train the synapses that you want to fire together to wire together.

WHAT YOU'LL GET OUT OF THE 30-DAY CHALLENGE

When you commit to following the Radical Vision Challenge for thirty days, you have already made a massive change in the way your brain maps your reality. Remember, knowing and becoming are interwoven.

You will be developing the mental culture that converts limiting beliefs and emotions to empowering beliefs and emotions.

And, most importantly, you will be taking immediate, massive, and measured action toward your Radical Vision. This will bring you closer to the point where your vision becomes a magnet that pulls you toward it, rather than you having to fight the inertia generated by great change.

SO ARE YOU READY TO CHANGE YOUR LIFE?

DO YOU HAVE THE SUPPORT OF THE PERSONAL EVOLUTION TRIBE?

Step 1: Join the Personal Evolution Tribe here: https://www.facebook.com/groups/personalevolutiontribe

Step 2: Go to www.personalevolutionplan.com and download the 30-Day Radical Vision Challenge Quick Start Kit. The infographic and customizable AVID journal will provide you with all the tools you need to get started.

Step 3: Plan your first "Flow Day" tomorrow

Commit to waking up twenty minutes earlier and going through the anchoring and visualizing process outlined in Chapter 12 and online in the Personal Evolution Plan.

During your day, remain mindful of the decisions you're making, the actions you're taking, and whether these are in alignment with your Positive Core. Check in once a day with The Personal Evolution Tribe on Facebook and share an insight from the day. I'll be there personally to guide with provocative questions.

Finally, commit to taking an extra twenty minutes before bed to go through the debrief process outlined in Chapter 10 and online in Personal Evolution Plan.

That's it, twenty minutes in the morning, twenty minutes at night, and being mindful during the day.

Step 4: Find an accountability partner (if you need one)

Throughout the book, we've discussed the importance of community. The Personal Evolution Tribe is there for your support, accountability, and to improve the people in your Top Five (remember we're the average of the five people we spend the most time with). Make sure to go to https://www.facebook.com/groups/personalevolutiontribe and get connected with the amazing people who are changing the world and manifesting their Radical Visions!

Final Advice: Don't wait!

Start now. Do not allow time to pass before taking action on your 30-day challenge. This is how people remain stuck in the status quo. The difference between everybody in the unhappy, unfulfilled, and disengaged majority and the small percentage of people living lives of abundant mastery is that the latter group takes immediate action. Who are you going to be?

PLEASE LET ME KNOW HOW I CAN ADD VALUE TO YOU

I wish you the best of luck on your hero's journey. If there is any way at all that I can support you, please let me know.

CONTACT ME ANYTIME

I am always eager to connect with like-minded people. If you have questions or just want to reach out to me, please feel free to do so. I'd love to connect with you. Just go to WWW.MIKEMERRIAM.COM and click the Contact tab to send me a message. I'm looking forward to hearing from you.

PAY IT FORWARD

Can you do me a special favor?

If you enjoyed this book and took value from it, perhaps you feel there's someone in your life who may also benefit from it. If so, let them borrow your copy, give it to them, or better yet, get them their own copy. Closer Than You Think makes a great holiday or birthday gift, or is appropriate just as a token of love and friendship.

Your friends and family can also go to WWW.MIKEMERRIAM.COM and download the first two chapters of the book for free.

ADVANCED OPPORTUNITIES

To book me to speak at your event, go to WWW.MIKEMERRIAM. COM and click the Speaking tab.

For information on private one-on-one coaching or group coaching with me, go to WWW.MIKEMERRIAM.COM and click the Coaching tab.

BONUS MATERIALS

Because I'm so thankful that you've taken the time to purchase and read my book, I wanted to leave you with a little bonus. I've put a lot of time into setting and accomplishing goals in my life. I use a fairly straightforward framework that's built on the old acronym of SMART combined with the 80/20 rule of essentialism, also known as the Pareto Principal. This rule asserts that 80 percent of outcomes are driven by 20 percent of actions. It can be applied universally in life. I try to live my life with the understanding that only about 20 percent of anything is meaningful. The rest is distraction.

Anyway, I hope you enjoy my structure for setting and accomplishing goals. I've given you a couple of personal examples to give you greater understanding of my process.

MIKE'S GOAL FRAMEWORK

There's an age-old acronym around setting goals that most of us probably learned in school somewhere along the line. It's as true today as it ever was then, when it comes to setting goals in a way designed to actually accomplish them.

SMART — Specific, Measurable, Attainable, Relevant, Time-Bound

When setting your goals, always make sure each of these important factors is addressed within your goal. For example, my goal around this book was as follows:

Finish writing my book by June 1st, 2016 and launch it on Amazon by August 8th. Become a #1 bestseller and leverage this to launch a business teaching individuals and organizations to become the best versions of themselves, thus adding my greatest value to the world.

My goal met all of the SMART metrics. It was very specific, measurable, attainable, relevant to me, and had a time limit. Because my goal was SMART, I was able to outline the essential priorities and actions that I needed to take to give myself the best chance of accomplishing my goal. (Note: I missed the timing on this goal, but I did eventually accomplish it).

One final piece of advice on goals, as one of my mentors Jon Berghoff told me, your goals themselves are less important than how you engage them. Meaning, the language you use, the responses you choose, the decisions you make, and the actions you take are what matter. The goal can be anything, but engaging it properly is what moves you forward.

Make sure you can see your goals. See the big picture. Visualize them and see the entire pathway. Then see them as already accomplished while you're going through the process of taking your essential actions. Most importantly, express gratitude for what you will accomplish as though you've already accomplished it. This can literally trick your brain into thinking you have. Just make sure your body knows it still needs to act!

Let's walk through an example of how to establish a goal, break it down into its components, and then identify the essential functions and actions necessary to accomplish it.

First: Write down a goal (the easy part).

Once your goal is written down, the next step is to figure out how to get started. This requires you to breakdown the goal into its components to better understand the nature of each component and give you the daily actions that need to be taken.

The following is one of my goals that I outlined while working in the mortgage industry.

Goal: Fund $25 Million in Mortgage Loans (120 units) in 2015, working 25 hours per week.

Question - Is this goal SMART?

- Specific: Yes — Fund $25 million in loans working 25 hours per week.
- Measurable: Yes — This should take 120 units or 10 units per month.
- Attainable: Yes — I've come close to this number in the past.
- Relevant: Yes — I'm experienced and well connected in the industry.
- Time-Bound: Yes — In the year 2015.

Breakdown Goal: Fund $25 Million in Mortgage Loans (120 units) in 2015, working 25 hours per week.

- 10 units per month – 2.25 units per week – Considering a 40 percent loss rate (60 percent capture) that's four units per week.

- Working five hours per day, I need to capture a lead every 6.15 hours. Essentially, one per day.
- Create a streamlined system to not lose time processing.

Essential Functions: These are the top three functions that generate the highest level of success in funding mortgage loans. Otherwise known as the "money making activities" or the 80/20 Rule.

- Networking for loans
- Managing the process to best efficiency
- Communicating with clients and partners

Essential Actions: Breakdown the essential functions into actions.

- Networking for loans
- Call all of my existing real estate agents every week (Monday).
- Call new five new real estate agents every week (Tuesday).
- Go see my builder reps every week (Wednesday).
- Managing the process to best efficiency
- Spend the time with processors and assistants to improve their level of competence and confidence.
- Track the milestones.
- Communicating with clients and partners
- Updates to real estate agents every week (Monday).
- Updates to customers every week (Thursday).

This is just one example of a goal I set. This particular goal was related to something that I was already doing, funding mortgage loans on a high level. Perhaps your goal is to start something completely new that you aren't currently involved in. Your goal breakdown may look something like this:

Your Example Goal: Start a new online marketing business within three months that will allow me to quit my job within eighteen months of launch.

Breakdown Goal: Start a new online marketing business within three months that will allow me to quit my job within eighteen months of launch.

Question - Is this goal SMART?

- Specific: Yes — Start a new online marketing business.
- Measurable: Yes — Within three months.
- Attainable: Yes — You're not claiming you will climb Mt. Everest in the next three months. An online marketing business should be doable.
- Relevant: Yes — Assuming you have some knowledge in this arena.
- Time-Bound: Yes — Quit my job within eighteen months.

How do I Start? (Write down some questions and answers, and then use the answers to define next steps.)

- What problem am I solving?
- Who else is currently working in this space? What are they doing well? Where are there opportunities to improve?
- Define my target audience (Avatar).
- How will I deliver my service to them?

Essential Functions: What are the top three things essential to starting an online marketing business?

- Research and develop idea into a business plan
- Build an audience by increasing online presence
- Integrate online profiles and platforms to maximize communications reach

Essential Actions: Breakdown essential functions into actions.

- Research and develop idea into a business plan
- Write a description of my company.
- Perform a market analysis.
- Outline marketing strategy.
- Run financial projections.
- Build an audience by increasing online presence
- Write blog posts.
- Invest in advertisements.
- Integrate online profiles and platforms to maximize communications reach
- Create a Facebook page and group.
- Generate a call to action.

This format for setting and accomplishing goals is simple and easy to follow. What's not so simple is holding yourself accountable. Making sure you're actually doing the things you say you want to do.

A SPECIAL INVITATION

You are cordially invited to join our growing private tribe of Radical Visioneers, thought-leaders, and like-minded personal evolutionaries, all dedicated to massively transformative futures.

Just go to https://www.facebook.com/groups/personalevolutiontribe/ and request to join.

This book is evergreen, meaning it lives electronically online. Because of this, it can be updated at any time. I'm hoping we can work together to update it in the future.

I'm inviting you to join me in answering the following questions:

What would it look like if this book became *the book* to achieve a radically transformative future filled with unlimited happiness and fulfillment?

How could we add to, subtract from, and/or adapt this book so that it becomes the *ultimate guide* and *go-to resource?*

I'm inviting you to join me in answering these questions and making this a reality. I'm looking forward to seeing you in The Personal Evolution Tribe. I'm committed to collaborating in an effort to build great ideas, work to improve lives, and change the world together.

I have a vision to change the world one Personal Evolution at a time. Will you join this me?

ACKNOWLEDGMENTS

Every person that I've ever come into contact with has something to do with who I am today, and therefore I would like to thank everybody who has ever crossed my path for your interaction. Whether it was positive, negative, or indifferent, I could not be exactly where I am right now without you, and I love exactly where I am right now. So thank you!

To the people who have had a more direct impact on my life, I cannot thank you enough for the love, support, and inspiration I draw from each of you.

To my wife Melissa, the dedication of this book says it all. I would not, could not, and will not live my radical future without you!

To my twin boys, Declan and Ronan, you are my truest inspiration. Thank you so much for teaching me what it's like to love others so significantly more than I love myself. You are the greatest gift in my life and you always will be. Because I love you so much, I have agreed to also list our dog Hunter in here. Are you happy now? (They're standing over my shoulder as type to make sure I thank the dog!)

To my parents, Marty and Diane Merriam, your unconditional love, guidance, and support throughout my life has instilled a level of confidence in me that empowers me to go after my dreams.

Thank you so much for being there for me, for setting such a strong example, and for filling me with the love and confidence that allow me to thrive. You are responsible for the operating system that allows me to thrive.

To my sister, Lisa Young, I am so proud of you. Your entrepreneurial journey is an inspiration to me, and I'm looking forward to traveling on the path to greatness alongside you as you continue to build your business, and I build mine.

To my friend and brother-in-law, Jim Young, thank you for always believing in me and being a great friend.

To my niece, Hanna Young, you are proof that we can learn valuable lessons from the youngest people in our lives just as easily as we can from our peers and elders. Your confidence, independence, willingness to be yourself and screw other people's judgments, and your sincere empathy for other people inspire me. You are part of a great generation, and I'm looking forward to seeing you become a leader.

To my brother from another mother, Erin Freize, thank you for your unconditional friendship for the past thirty years. I love you, brother.

To my friend and mentor, Scott Groves, my life began to change the moment I met you. You, my friend, are largely responsible for helping me find the path that I'm on. I can't thank you enough for inspiring me to up my output. Although I may never be able to match the incredible results and value you put out, I will never cease trying. Thank you for helping me expand my circle and being an example of authenticity. I can't wait to see what you do next!

To my coach, mentor, and friend, Hal Elrod, *The Miracle Morning*, has had the most positive impact on my life of any book I've ever read. It was during my own Miracle Morning that the vision for changing my life struck me, and the ideas in this book were formed. I can't thank you enough for the inspiration you've given me. You are changing lives on a level that I can only dream to emulate someday. Every time I think I've learned everything you have to teach, you show up with an unlimited amount more to give. Thank you for your work, thank you for your coaching, thank you for your support, and thank you for your friendship.

To my friend, coach, and mentor, Jon Berghoff, you are brilliant! So many of the ideas, principles, and techniques in this book were derived from listening to and working with you. You have quite literally been the most influential person in my personal growth. I cannot thank you enough for everything you have given and continue to give to me. Your authenticity and selfless leadership are an inspiration. Thank you for your guidance.

To John Lee Dumas of Entrepreneur on Fire, your show was and is a huge factor in my own development. I have listened every day for the past two years. I've been introduced to hundreds of entrepreneurs around the world through your platform and have been inspired by so many of them, as well as by your relentless pursuit of excellence. You are doing great work! Thank you so much.

To every member of my QLM Family, many of whom I'm building great friendships with, including Stephen Christopher, Scott Groves, Jon Berghoff, Hal Elrod, Jon Vroman, Scot Lowry, Nicole Keating, Jeremy "Brotha James" Reisig, Mike McCarthy, Lance Salazar, Alicia Messa, Andrew Smallwood, Carey Smolenski, Julian Landy, John Ruhlin, Julianna Raye, Mike Eaton, Tonya Rineer, Matt Aitchison, Lindsay McCarty, Matt Emery, Isaac Stegman, Greg Kelly, Brandy Salazar, Jeff Latham, Tim Rhode, Angie Macdougall, Susan Adams, Sharissa Malave, Jenna Bayne, Hector Santiesteban, Justin Grable, Tiffany Swineheart, Heidi Murray, Matt Graves, Megan Lyons, Nina Perez, Debra Wanger, Shannon Vanasse, Judi Finneran, Paul Cantu, Joe Perkins, Warren Macdougall, DonnaLisa Albini, Susan Rosengren, Alissa Nelson, Demi Wang, Josh Painter, Victor Ramirez, John Negrete, Stephen Putonti, Rebecca Denson, Tamas Perlaky, Mark Lui. Hope I spelled everyone's name right and didn't leave anyone out. You are all so important to me!

To all of the mentors and heroes that I haven't had the honor of meeting or working directly with but have inspired me through your work, both past and present, Jim Rohn, Tony Robbins, Tim Ferriss, Zig Ziglar, Napoleon Hill, Stephen Covey, Deepak Chopra, John Warrillow, Maharishi Mahesh Yogi, and John C Maxwell, just to name a few, you are the giants whose shoulders everyone who desires to change the world stands on.

Finally, to you, the reader, you are amazing. You have the ability to change the world. Thank you for allowing me to be a part of your life. I'm looking forward to connecting with you in the Personal Evolution Tribe. Please do not hesitate to reach out to me if I can add value to your world. Thank you for reading my book. I can't wait to see you living your radial vision! Remember to empower others to do the same.

Made in the USA
Middletown, DE
12 December 2016